CHRIST THE TIGER

Thomas Howard

CHRIST

*A Postscript
to Dogma*

THE

TIGER

J. B. LIPPINCOTT COMPANY
Philadelphia and New York

For Lovelace
who became for me
as a figure of theotokos

The word within a word, unable to speak a word,
Swaddled with darkness. In the juvescence of the year
Came Christ the tiger

T. S. Eliot, "Gerontion"

Preface

Things have a way of falling to pieces. The shingles blow off the roof. The fender rusts through and the exhaust pipe drags. Cuffs fray, nylons run, hair falls out, joints stiffen, and wattles appear under our chins. Nothing is exempt, not even our ideas.

Athens begins with a great and democratic vision, and finishes in ruin and ignominy. Arthur begins with a high vision of a knightly fellowship, and it all ends in perfidy. Washington and Jefferson have an exhilarating idea for a new kind of nation, and it progresses to the tumidity and bathos of the Great Society.

Political vision is not alone in this wry tendency. The highest of all ideas, religious dogma, is subject to the assault of time and evil. There was a noble law for human intercourse given at Sinai, and within a few hundred years it had deteriorated at the hands of its practitioners to a cynical array of functions. There was a new and energetic law announced in Judah, and within a few centuries it had calcified into a brittle and gorgeous *objet d'art*. The process is not only historic. It occurs in one's own consciousness. We begin with something which we take to be pure and inviolable, and within a few years we find ourselves a thousand miles from where we began.

This is especially so in the case of someone who is born into a tradition of dogmatic orthodoxy, no matter what that particular orthodoxy is. (Let it be noted here that the terms "dogmatic" and "orthodoxy" are not pejorative: "dogmatic" implies simply the reference to a system of thought, whether that be Keynesian economics or radical egalitarianism; "orthodoxy" implies the effort to keep your dogma intact—that is, to keep it in its early form.) A person in this situation begins life with a set of certainties that accounts for everything. It is axiomatic that his tradition is the correct one. It is also understood that his particular *sector* of his tradition is the only pure one.

Then he stumbles out into the great glittering world. He is threatened and dazzled and frightened and intoxicated. There is more occurring in human existence than he had thought. There are compelling alternatives to his certainties. There are obvious rewards to be had by simply leaving his categories behind.

In one form or another, this is the experience of a great many people. The process of becoming adult seems often to involve the corollary process of disavowing not only one's childhood, but everything attached to it.

This book is the story of one man's experience. The dogmatic orthodoxy was that of Christianity in its conservative Protestant form.

There is, however, one odd note: as of this writing, I have not done the expected thing. I have not disavowed Christianity. The pulling and hauling has not convinced me that God was *not* in Christ. It has, on the other hand, led me to suspect that we are involved in something wild and unmanageable, and in nothing that can be successfully incarcerated in any dogmatic orthodoxy.

I have a friend who, in any discussion about any topic at all, intones with liturgical regularity, "That's where the whole thing breaks down." She is usually right. For there is a point, or a thousand points in any system, at which that system is mortally vulnerable.

This is one reason why I find the Incarnation compelling. For in the figure of Jesus the Christ there is something that escapes us. He has been the subject of the greatest efforts at systematization in the history of man. But anyone who has ever tried this has had, in the end, to admit that the seams

9

keep bursting. He sooner or later discovers that he is in touch, not with a pale Galilean, but with a towering, and furious figure who will not be managed.

Part 1

One way of describing my childhood would be to say that it was a massive effort to get cozy. My earliest recollection is of myself down under the covers of my crib, blanket clips and all, during my afternoon nap. My mother had a renown of sorts for having contrived the perfect nightgown for babies, with a very long skirt and a draw-string in the bottom hem to be tied around one of the struts at the end of the crib. This gives the baby freedom to move around, but prevents his plunging over the sides, or crawling out of the covers and freezing. This way the baby stays warm, and mother isn't up and down all night long wondering if the covers are still on.

In any case, I began in a cozy way, and kept trying to stay cozy. I wanted things to be safe and

11

warm and tidy. I remember once spending a long time arranging meticulously on a table top a great array of my trinkets, and it was to my dismay that I was told that this would not do. They were better off back in their drawers. But I liked the look of them sitting there in rows.

I had a yellow tricycle, and I used to get a pleasant sensation when I would stoop down to work in the supposed engine and would feel the warmth of the sidewalk near me. I liked the sunlight coming through the great tulip poplar tree, down onto the concrete, and the feeling that I was down there where I could not fall.

An early trauma occurred in kindergarten. One afternoon the teacher, Miss Purcell, asked us if we would rather cut out valentines or listen to a story. I was entirely alone in begging for a story. "Valentines! Valentines!" shouted the whole class. I can remember the others' brisk enthusiasm over the idea. But valentines represented to me a chaos of paste, scissors, noise, and, worst of all, competition. "What a lovely valentine Katherine has made!" and I knew I would look at my own pinched and humped hearts and realize that they were dismal failures. If we could only curl up on our blankets (we had blankets) for a story. The quietness, the tranquillity, and the teacher's voice leading us into some marvellous never-never land. But no.

At home, my mother had read the Pooh books to me, and I had liked sitting on the porch hearing about the warm and sunny spot on the edge of the Hundred Acre Wood where Kanga took Roo to play, or listening to Mother sing "Go Tell Aunt Nancy," or "I Went to Visit a Friend One Day." One song that had pierced my consciousness with shafts from some gothic and twilit realm and that filled me with infinite awe and sadness was about Five Brave Knights. I visualized them coming out of a dark wood of conifers, across a green, green sward and past an open casement window where a princess sat. Baseball stories, dog stories, horse stories, and sea stories left me cold. But knights and forests and spells and castles suggested a world I felt I must one day discover.

When I was seven, we moved around the corner to a house that had only fifteen (instead of eighteen) rooms. It was a nicer house, though. The front door closed with a thick sound, and did not rattle like the glass-windowed door in the other house. My brother and I had double-decker beds in a small room on the northeast side of the house, where the worst weather comes from in South Jersey. This was something of a challenge to our resourcefulness in making the room safe from tempest. (I think my brother shared the idea of coziness; whether this was prenatal or fraternal influence, I do not know.) On Saturday mornings we would tuck a blanket along the edge of the upper bunk, making a curtained recess of his bed, and, gathering our menage of stuffed animals, and a huge pile

13

of Beatrix Potter books, we would ride out the Nor'-easters that slashed against the storm windows outside.

On clear Saturdays we would get the express wagon from the garage, load it up with peach baskets, old blankets, rakes, shovels, and other equipment, and set off on forays around the driveway. Or we would help my father spread ashes from the coal furnace out on the cinder driveway in the ruts washed out by the rain. I think I saw in all of this a shoring up of things against nature, ambiguity, decay, and the unknown. I doubt if I phrased it that way, however.

Once when we had all been to one of our favorite swimming places in the Jersey pines for the day, we drove into a ditch as we started home. I was desperate. To see that familiar, comfortable gray 1941 Plymouth at a forty-five degree angle in a sandy rut was too much. I knew the end was at hand. I was wild with fright. The men who came along with a truck and a rope seemed like angels from God.

Once my aunt organized a small daytime outing to the far end of town. She and my grandfather and one or two others would go in the car to an ice-cream parlor, and I would follow on my bike. I understood this to mean that the two vehicles would travel along the street together. It went well for a few blocks, but when we got on toward the edge of town, I realized that the car was moving farther and farther away from me. I pedaled furiously, waving and calling out, and beginning to sob in rage and terror. They waved back from the disappearing car. I finally gave it up and rode home in agony. My mother, to cheer me up, gave me a nickel for a Coke at the drugstore, and for some reason I sat down in a booth and not the counter. I waited for what seemed an eternity, trying to catch the eyes of the chattering girls behind the counter. I failed and again rode home. I could not find it in me to go to the counter and *ask* for service. I thought there was some mocking conspiracy among the waitresses to ignore me. It turned out later that my aunt had meant for us all to rendezvous at the end of the trip and that they had interpreted my signaling as a cheery wave.

I had an afternoon paper route for several years. Delivering the papers to forty or more porches became routine, and I used to fill the time by telling myself stories. These went on for days, and the general thrust of most of them seems to have been to get and keep things safe. I made up murder stories, and Crusoe-like tales of intrepidity, and endless tales built around the idea of huge stores of provisions. In fact, most of the plots were the merest frames for elaborate descriptions of forts or storerooms or wine cellars or ships' holds. Everyone was always storing up things against weather or time or the enemy. Once, in first grade, I had crayoned a picture of a dairy. There were a minuscule man and a cow at the bottom of the picture, and the rest of the space was filled with an enormous yellow rectangle. It was a great block of butter. One never knows when the supply of butter may run out.

For several years I dreamed of raising poultry. I subscribed to the *Poultry Tribune* and went often to help an elderly gentleman farmer with his chickens. I indulged in endless fancies and drew innumerable diagrams of how my poultry farm would look. Its main features were coziness and vast supplies of laying mash. The farmhouse and the chicken house would be under one roof, and everything would be warm and clean and safe. I am sure that both I and my chickens would have died of suffocation had my plan ever matured.

Even consumer products either supported or threatened my world. My mother, for instance, used Crisco shortening, and the tins of Spry on our neighbors' shelves looked hostile to me. We used Bon Ami scouring powder, and there seemed to be something sinister about the old woman on the can of Dutch Cleanser. We had a Plymouth, and I always thought of Fords as hard and worldly cars. (You could tell this from the noise of the starter: Plymouths started with a comfortable huff, while Fords started with a metallic scurry, like someone scraping a tack over a copper screen.) My mother shopped at an old grocery store called Matlack's. It was owned by two brothers. I liked the soft, scuffed floor boards, the wooden counter, and the complicated tongs on the end of a long pole that they used to snatch down cans from high shelves. At the other end of Main Street, however, was another grocery store called Wolfe's, and I was sure no family we knew ever bought their groceries there. Our baker was the Dugan man, and I did not like the look of the Bond and Freihofer trucks.

Life at our house ran meticulously. My mother and father both would rather have erred on the side of being an hour early than five minutes late. My father was out of bed by 5:30 in the morning and followed an unalterable pattern of personal devotions, shaving, dressing, and breakfast for, as far as I know, more than thirty years. My mother, who did not share this zest for the dawn, heroically rose at 6:30, and we all had breakfast at seven. At 6:55 my brother and I would hear a table knife tapping on the steampipe that came up through the kitchen to our radiator. It was time to start down the stairs. This punctuality never quite rubbed off on my brother, and the rest of us would often be well into breakfast before we realized that there was total silence in the bedroom overhead. It usually turned out that he was contemplating a shoe, or looking at one of the water colors in the Potter books. He is an artist.

At the end of breakfast we went to the living room for prayers. A hymn, with my mother at the piano, a section from the Bible, and prayer, ending with the Lord's Prayer. Then I practiced the piano for twenty minutes before my neighbor Billy Hall came to the porte-cochere with his bicycle and called me for school. It infuriated me when my sister would summon me back from the piano to the kitchen to eat my crusts and finish my juice. I felt that she was taking advantage of the dubious authority implied in her eighteen months' seniority.

Young children in my religious tradition probably become more familiar with the content of the Old and New Testaments than most doctors of theology. It is a painless education, in that it is part of the stuff of daily life and conversation, so that I early became familiar with Jael, Sisera, Gehazi, Hagar, Ehud, Maher-shalal-hashbaz, Eutychus, and Eunice. I also became a master of hymnology. My father inclined neither to the jejune attempts at hymnody by recent Protestantism, nor to the treacly sentiments of Gospel choruses. So we sang "the great hymns of the church" at prayers. By the time I was twelve, I suppose I had memorized all four verses of hundreds of hymns, without any conscious effort at all. I acquired through them a fairly measured, historically oriented, non-lunatic-fringe view of God, and of what faith and devotion imply.

Two of my favorite places were my father's study at home, and his office in Philadelphia. His study was a small room at the back of the house. Its walls were lined with books. On the desk top there were

18

long yellow pencils, and a brass duck head whose bill would open on a spring and snap onto letters, and a row of books, and a reading stand, and a clock. When it was not in his waistcoat pocket, his thin black leather notebook lay flat on the desk next to the pencils. I liked to see him take it from his pocket and flip it open in one motion like the fastest gun in the West. The orange lining with its tiny pocket containing a laminated card-sized calendar and a Pennsylvania Railroad commuter schedule, and some notes, seemed to bespeak a world that was manageable.

I knew that in this study, every morning, my father opened his Bibles and commentaries and ancient books of devotion, and that he prayed for all of us, and for all of his friends, and, on given days of the week, for items in his own personality. On one day he would pray for patience, and on another for courage, and on another for peace. Sometimes, when I came down early in the morning, I would see him sitting there in his chair, or kneeling by it, with his blue wool bathrobe on and an afghan over his shoulders. He had a particular early morning look, without his collar and tie on, and with his hair still dry and tousled from bed.

From time to time my mother would take us into Philadelphia to "the office." It was an enclave of familiarity in the dirty bustle of the city. Good things occurred here. It was the center of focus for a world-wide enterprise. All over the world there were people who thought a great deal of what went on at 325 North 13th St.

The neighborhood could not have been worse. The office was on the sixth floor of a loft building. There were umbrella factories and other obscure enterprises on the lower floor. Across the street was the morgue. I used to watch police cars and limousines pulling up to the front door, loading and unloading weeping women, and hearses and panel trucks pulling up to a platform in a side alley, loading and unloading corpses. Usually these were in wicker baskets or on covered stretchers. Once I watched two policemen fling a stiffened nude old man from a rolling table onto a low stretcher. At intervals the air in the neighborhood took on a peculiar acrid smell, and office speculation was that the excess stock across the street was being incinerated.

The children in our family were celebrities of a sort in the office, in that my grandfather was the president of the company, and my father was the editor (it was a religious journal). We ran a gantlet of exclaiming switchboard operators, accountants, and secretaries en route from the elevator to my father's office, and I felt that I enjoyed this. I was especially impressed with one woman who wore her hair swept up into curls on the top of her head and used a bit of lipstick and, I think, rouge. I was not sure what religious view to take of this (make-up was deprecated in our world), but she was an excessively pleasant woman.

20

I liked to reach up to the tiny blackened brass frog knocker on my father's office door to let him know we had arrived. He sat, tall and straight in his white shirt behind his desk facing the door. It was a miserable office, I am sure, but I never saw this until years later. I liked the pads of paper and the In and Out boxes and the Ediphone and the glass-doored bookcases.

Once a year I would spend a day in this office, and my father would take me around to visit the proofreaders and secretaries, and then back to the composing room. The linotype operator would make lead slugs with my name on them, and an old mustachioed Scot with a spittoon would show me how to read type in reverse. I felt that the composing room was one of the eternal verities. It had been there forever, and would remain forever. I was not as sure of the pressroom. It was in the basement, and I was not at all sure that the men down there were Christians.

What I liked was a world that was familiar and predictable, and one that shared a commonalty of beliefs and sensibility with me. I found this at home and in the office. I felt that I ought to find it above all at church.

We went to a small church whose congregation did not represent the local Blue Book. This was during an era when Protestantism had given up the traditional Christian description of things and was trying to arrive at a concordat with the modern world in non-supernaturalistic terms. It was a pro-

21

longed attempt, and a courageous one, but the view backwards now is that they lost both their creed and the world. In any case, our group held to what it saw to be Biblical Christianity, and protested the mass apostasy of the age.

Here were people, I thought, who are going to heaven as I am. I was part of this embattled, faithful minority. Surely they were my people. But I found that the bleakest hours of the week were those spent in Sunday School and Young People's. I knew that what was being taught here was true, and that these people were good and the rest of the world bad. But I could not feel any zest for it.

For one thing, I was fastidious. Some of the church members were from farms, and some were from poor neighborhoods, and I was not successful in bridging this gap. I was not able to resolve the difficulty arising in my mind over the juxtaposition of godliness and body odor. I saw other people who apparently had no consciousness of distinctions in dress and taste, and I sometimes wished for this brisk approach to life, but I was paralyzed by reflection and by my nostrils. I gagged over the green tartar on my Sunday School classmates' teeth, and over their black and bitten half-moon fingernails, and ears filled with dark orange wax.

My image of godliness was a clear one. My father, my grandfather, and my great-uncle, who were important figures in our wing of Christendom, were august, cultivated, articulate gentlemen. The names in my father's list of saints and heroes of the faith were like this too: William Law, Jeremy Taylor, George Whitefield, Bishop Handley Moule, and John Wesley. When I thought of myself forty years hence, I saw a tall, gracious, intelligent gentleman, shaking hands kindly with adoring middle-aged women who had just heard me speak, or knew me from my writings. I somehow got images of the British Empire and turn-of-the-century dress and great houses mixed in with it all.

I felt that I possessed an array of data that accounted for every possible phenomenon of the world and experience. I had a specific set of desiderata before my eyes. I felt myself a part of an almost invisible minority which had the saving truth for the world. I felt that there was divine sanction for every item and procedure in our tradition. I felt that there was a language whereby alone one could describe the world and history. Life posed a threat to my being and to my creed, and I feared the onslaught of Jews, Turks, infidels, and heretics. I regretted the actualities of the flesh. There were a great many areas of experience to be deplored. The great thing was to get on to Paradise in as unscathed a condition as possible.

I felt that if one could trim down one's world to a manageable size, it would be a good thing. I wanted to exclude the unfamiliar and the distasteful. The Nor'easters outside the bedroom window, the valentine competition, the wolves outside the chicken house, the liberals in the big churches, the Catholics and Jews and Negroes—one had to have defenses.

*

I went to a Quaker day school for the first three years of grammar school. The first and second grades were housed in a small white frame building. We had a fireplace and a carpet, and the teacher read stories to us. In the third grade, we were moved to the big brick high school building. In fourth grade, I was transferred to the public school: the Quakers were introducing into their curriculum various views of the world that my parents felt were hardly nonpartisan. They were teaching Darwinism, not as theory, but as history. At public school there was a one-acre cinder playground instead of twenty acres of green grass as we had had at Friends' School. There were one thousand students instead of three hundred. And there were children from across the tracks.

When I was a sophomore in high school I went away to school in Florida. I cried bitterly into my pillow, night after night, thinking about the Saturday mornings at home, and supper in the kitchen, and the shops along Main Street. I could not accept the idea of irrecoverability. During my junior year, my sister, who was probably the closest person in the world to me, visited me on her way to South America as a missionary, and when she drove away from the campus, I felt that my world had collapsed. If only we could turn time back just a tiny bit. But it had slipped by now, and there was no way of ever recovering things that meant more to me than all the world.

The school was a sequestered one, and I was able to develop a perspective on things while I was there. I believed that what God wanted was men who would be willing to burn out for Him. If He had gone to the great length of dying for me, and had endured the agony and bloody sweat, the nails and the scoffing and obloquy, what did He ask of me? Surely to abandon the things of time and sense, and all the ambitions that men hold dear—education, position, influence, money, fame, bliss—and to pour out my life for Him as He had poured out His for me. Men around me were perishing. What did it matter in the light of eternity whether or not my name ever got into the history books or the society page? We were pilgrims and strangers here. Our forebears were Moses and Jeremiah and John the Baptist and Christ—all of them outcasts and failures.

I came to feel that the great thing was to have a singleness of vision. We must do God's work, and this work was to fill up the gaps through which men were tumbling to perdition. I heard about a vision that a great woman had had once of hordes plunging over a cliff and of people who might have rescued them sitting in a meadow nearby making daisy chains. I found this imagery compelling. Obviously most of the things that occupy men's attention are daisy chains.

There were several Biblical injunctions that operated in my thinking at this period. I thought about "Let us lay aside every weight and the sin which doth so easily beset us." This takes in a great deal, I thought. Not only sins (perfidy and cynicism and lust and so on) but *weights*. This must mean things which are otherwise good, but which an athlete can't take with him. Others are free to wear attractive clothes. An athlete strips down. Others may have coffee and cake and chocolates with impunity. A runner eats proteins and vegetables. I thought about Daniel who ate pulse (I did not know what pulse was, but it sounded spiritual) while everyone else ate the king's food, and of Samson's Nazarite vow, excluding himself from otherwise legitimate things. I often pictured myself on my knees in a grass hut in Central Africa, with my Bible on my cot in front of me, pouring out my life in prayer and agony before God for the souls of the people to whom I had been sent. Let others pursue the foxfire of success. Let them have their split-level houses and cars and junior executive fedoras and beige wall-to-wall carpeting. This was all vain, fatuous, and futile. God, just let me be your pioneer. I liked

St. Paul's "Woe unto me if I preach not the Gospel." And I liked to think about the Suffering Servant, who "set his face like a flint" to do God's will. God needed people who would narrow down their focus to one thing: rescuing souls. I developed a vision of godliness, then, that involved ardor, sacrifice, and simplicity. Contrary to this I saw a vision of "the world." I developed this latter vision, not from the Bible, as I had done with my idea of godliness, but from popular hearsay. In this vision, the world implied sex, alcohol, tobacco, bridge, the fox trot, the races, and the movies. It was a highly specific vision and therefore eminently manageable. The threat of evil dwindled in so far as I was able to locate it and isolate it. It helped support my consciousness of my own progress in godliness to know that at least I was halfway along the road by virtue of having renounced "the world"—i.e., my list.

Despite my program of ascetic zeal, I was not unaware of my own iniquities. I knew that I wanted other people's lips and bodies madly, and I felt that my ways of compensating for the lack of actual physical involvement were to be deplored. I suspected also that I was a pompous prig and that, in so far as I spoke of my own experience of God, I was being cynical. I thought about the white rage of which I was capable, which few people had really seen. I had cursed God elaborately and foully a thousand times in my silent furies. But this was all the sort of thing one could keep under one's hat, as it were. In the meantime, I avoided things on the index.

I was swamped with dismay when I went to college. Here I encountered people who were from my own religious tradition, but who did not always appear to share my vision of godliness. I began on the assumption that they were unspiritual. As I was registering, I saw one of the athletic coaches, a burly, tanned, bald man who did not at all fit into my picture of what a Christian ought to look like. My classmates, in their scramble for popularity and class office, were clearly worldly, and had much to learn about piety.

I used to watch some of the social arbiters in my class driving in to Chicago on Friday and Saturday nights, with their striped ties, herringbone jackets, and button-down shirts. This is all mere sophistication, I thought. I am better off with my old starched collars and baggy gabardine slacks. Had not Jesus said "Take no thought what ye shall wear"?

I found my friends among a number of people with views like mine, and we organized a happy fellowship. One boy, clearly in earnest about godliness, was a Presbyterian. This confused me. Why had he not left this great and apostate church? Once at the supper table I threw him into high dudgeon by observing that the Presbyterian minister in my home town was not even *saved*. (I had concluded this on the basis of the general nature of the church there, which was not oriented to the same array of Biblical emphases as was ours). My friend would not go on until I had backed down. But I felt that he was truckling. I could not understand why he allied himself with organized Christendom, which was obviously a cadaver.

My group spent a great deal of time in the library studying. On week ends we spent quiet hours in our rooms in meditation and prayer or in little fellowship meetings. We liked the idea of all-night prayer meetings. There were crosscurrents even in this group, however, and some of the boys who were particularly attracted by the idea of charismatic phenomena began to look on the rest of us as unwilling to abandon everything, even reason and respectability and caution, for God. We, for our part, wondered what the limits of Christian enthusiasm were.

I developed further my set of religious foci during this period. I concentrated on scriptural ideas like this: "Keep thy heart with all diligence, for out of it are the issues of life," and "If I regard iniquity in my heart, the Lord will not hear me," and "Behold, thou desirest truth in the inward parts." One's attention, then, was to be inward. Christ had assailed the religious doctors of His day for being sepulchres, white on the outside, but full of rotting bones and putrefaction on the inside. The way to avoid this externalism, I felt, was to adopt devotional practices of a high order of intensity. I began to rise at 5:15 in the morning to pray and read my Bible. I tried to read every line in Scripture as applicable to myself that morning, whether it were David calling down a pox on his enemies, or Lot's daughters seducing him, or St. John's description of the pale horse.

A number of schools of religious thought presented themselves to me, but I felt that I was falling between all the stools there were.

There were, for instance, some groups of religious activists on campus toward which I never felt any attraction. One set of senior men had opted for a vigorous type of religion in which the idea was to win crowds of converts by sheer enthusiasm. There were bow ties and trumpet ensembles and jokes and whirlwind week-end trips in cars to churches furnished in blond wood, coral plastic upholstery, and electronic organs. One of my friends from this set said to me once, "God gets things done. He gets people saved." I felt guilty for not being a soul-winner, since in this religious tradition the propagation of the faith is to be carried on day and night, in all personal contacts, by every Christian. It makes sense. If you have a rope and someone is going over the cliff, you give him the rope. Or, if you have an exciting possession, you want to share it with your friends. This line of thought convinced me. The trouble was that I could not at all bring myself to open my mouth to non-Christians on the subject of Christ. My few efforts to do so were ghastly failures. I had seen my father, by nature a reticent person, talk to gas-station attendants and waitresses about Christ, and I knew it cost him dearly to do it. On the other hand, the father of one of my friends, who was a distinguished Washington banker, was able to talk with complete ease to every person he encountered and had a tally of hundreds of individual converts to his credit. What courage! What freedom! I wanted to be this kind of person.

Another group on campus comprised the cool, three-button tweed type. Their religion afforded them a very smart thing socially and at the same time a way of Christian service. Their approach to their clients was that it is possible to be a real cool kid and still be Christian. All the best people in the world are Christians. Or look at it the other way: Christians ought to be the coolest people around. None of the draggled, wispy, pimply, dandruff, Bible-packing sort of thing. Be the captain of your football team, be the fraternity president, be the head cheerleader, be the best dancer, but for God's sake take Jesus along for the ride. It's a ball.

One group that attracted me was English in its origin and had as its specialty something called "the victorious life." I had a genealogical interest in this, since it had been my great-uncle, among others, who had popularized the idea in America. I liked the atmosphere that surrounded this kind of thinking. These people were not inclined to displays of religious zeal and enthusiasm, but I felt that they had a deep taproot connecting them with spiritual realities that gave them their steadfastness and tranquillity. In order to have this victorious life, one had to "let go and let God." It was the simplest formula in the world. Do not try to do for yourself what Christ has already done for you. You are a failure. You cannot help but sin (*non posse non peccare*). But what do you suppose the Resurrection was all about? Christ rose a victor over sin as well as death, and now He lives *in* you. The entire power of the Resurrection is at your disposal. Stop trying to fight Satan and yourself with your silly little weapons. Go to the Victor. Christus Victor.

My own problem here was that, after years of attempting to let go, and repeated attempts to hunch myself over the fence into the green pasture, or even to let Christ get me over, I could not get there. I followed meticulously all the steps. I tried, and I tried not trying. I did everything the speakers told me to do and not to do. I finally concluded that I was not a candidate for the victorious life. Cupidity and my own consciousness had a way of staying alive, although I wanted desperately to believe that I had been crucified and risen with Christ.

Another syndrome seemed close to this one, and it fitted my inclination toward self-flagellation. The idea was to fix your gaze on the Cross. What would be the result? You would be broken. "Broken" was the operative word. This manifested itself publicly in confession meetings and prayer meetings. If we are truly broken before God, we will be broken before our brothers also, and the way to break yourself is to open yourself up. Tell your brother that you have harbored a grudge against him. Tell your sister in Christ that you have looked on her with lusting eyes. Tell the assembled company about your lies and your gossip and your passions. This will result in a healthy and open and free fellowship.

I felt frightened and condemned whenever I came under the influence of this sort of thing. I felt I must try to be broken, but I could never be enough of a spiritual nudist to succeed.

Several of my friends were eager to have re-enacted in their midst the phenomena described in the New Testament as having occurred at Pentecost. Although St. Paul issued strictures to the early Church about these things, he himself apparently had experienced the manifestations, and they seemed to be the key to great bursts of power and success spiritually. Great slices of Christendom are inquisitive about this sort of thing today, and I felt I might find something here.

A few of us drove to Chicago one night to an enormous church where a man gifted with healing and clairvoyant powers was to be preaching. We sat on the front row of the choir directly behind the pulpit, since the church was mobbed. For forty minutes before the man's arrival, we were encouraged to sing and pray and testify lustily. There was a great deal of noise, and I was prepared to see in it the freedom that comes when simple folk will open their hearts to the Holy Spirit and allow Him to blow with His wind through them. The man arrived, and spoke for perhaps an hour about some of the healing miracles of Jesus. Then people began to line up on the left of the platform, and the man would pray over each one, seizing their heads in his hands, and calling on God with great fervor. I looked eagerly at them as they went down from the platform. I had hoped to see crutches discarded and blind eyes restored and goiters dissolved. This did not occur. At this particular meeting the healing was directed to inner complaints—heart palpitations, stomach pains, shortness of breath, toothache.

I had not seen what I wanted, but I was not prepared to gainsay twenty centuries of experience from such disparate places as Jerusalem, Lourdes, Walsingham, and Texas, that God could heal people, and that He only waited to pour out his Pentecostal power on us all in healing and tongues. This quest never matured for me, in that I was not able to become sufficiently convinced that the apostles insisted that Pentecostal phenomena were a *sine qua non* for Christian experience.

Another group that engaged my attention for several years was one which felt that the great thing was to follow closely the apostolic order for Christian worship. They saw a great distance between the household meetings of the early Christians, and the glories of the Vatican, Canterbury, and Con-

34

stantinople, or even the tailored rigors of Geneva, Amsterdam, and Edinburgh. They sought to experience the equality and freedom before God which the first century Christians enjoyed. They understood clerisy and episcopacy to be unscriptural. The New Testament teaches that every Christian is a priest.

The care which these people exercised to avoid non-biblical accretions to Christian worship was matched by their care in observing Pauline order for the Church. Women were not permitted to speak at meetings where men were present, and must keep their heads covered. If there was to be a Bible study meeting in someone's home, the hostess would put her hat on for the hour. Women could speak to mixed groups via tape recorder, but not in person. At the Eucharist, there must be an unbroken loaf and a common cup, since this was presumably the case at the Last Supper. There were no clergy, synods, or curias. Each group was ruled directly by one or two local men who had no titles given to them. There was never any mistake, however, as to whom to see in a given group for instructions.

I was never able to penetrate this world. I had gold-plated family connections with them, and was even baptized by them while I was at college. But it was clear that they did not look on me as one of them, and I was made to understand this. Eventually my zest for re-enacting apostolic worship patterns withered.

One year an African clergyman from the Anglican Church visited the campus. I had a strange feeling about him. Here was someone who seemed to be a godly man and to whom I could not attach any stigmata of coldness, formalism, or idolatry, which was what I thought of in connection with the sacerdotal churches. I saw in him the meeting of two elements that I had thought were forever inimical: I had felt the Reformed and evangelical description of piety to be the great thing, but I had also, from my earliest years, had an almost erotic fascination with catholic Christendom. I was earnestly anti-Roman (and probably anti-Irish, anti-Italian, and anti-Polish to boot). But I had loved to hear my mother tell about her early years at St. Luke's Church Germantown, and about her beautiful and devout mother with her red leather Prayer Book and Hymnal. Once an Episcopal friend of mine took me into the church at home when we were boys. We stood in the dark nave, and I looked at the serene gray arches, and the gold and green altar covering, and the pulpit and lectern (I had never seen *two* desks in a church), and at the tiny prick of red from the ambry light, and I felt frightened and attracted. Once in New Hampshire I had contrived a Sunday outing to the Church of the Transfiguration in Bretton Woods for Evensong. I wanted to hear the boys' choir which sang there. I shall never forget that afternoon. I was at once in paradise and hell. I thought I had never seen and heard such beauty: the mountain valley, the brown-gray stone of the little church, the handsome congregation, the candles and crosses and dark wood, the beautiful faces of the choir boys, and the seraphic music. We sang "Saviour, Breathe an Evening Blessing," and, during the recessional, when I was in an agony, knowing that it was over, and that I would never see this again, we sang "Ten Thousand Times Ten Thousand." I was in a transport of grief, frenzy, and ecstasy. I felt that I had suddenly stumbled across something that had been there all along, and that I had missed. Something had pushed open the tiny door into the garden, and I would never be consolable after that glimpse. It all had something to do with beauty and loss and antiquity and irrevocability and desire and vision.

As a result of the African priest's visit to campus, a friend of mine returned to the Anglican Church. I began to accompany him to Morning Prayer on Sundays. I felt that I was betraying the simplicity of the Gospel and that I was seeking a sybaritic and aesthetic substitute for true religion. But I could not help myself. I wanted to find some validity for what I clearly loved.

At the beginning of my sophomore year, through the offices of an extremely popular girl who was a good friend, I was elected to the Student Council. My success was a mystery to me, in that I had, up to that point, been emphatically in a religious backwater on the campus. Who knew me? In any case, I moved into the world of campus politics. I was made a member of the "Spiritual Committee" of the Council. This was gratifying, as I felt that I was having an influence for good by being involved in discussions about chapel programs and prayer meetings.

At the end of that year I was persuaded to run for president of the Junior Class. I won the election, to the distinct horror of a number of articulate class members. Looking back now, I share their horror. I knew nothing at all about organizing enthusiasm, and class spirit, already moribund, died during my administration. We had a few flare-ups of hilarity, and I made an enormous new set of friends. But we did not succeed as a class.

Among my new friends were some of the football heroes and their girlfriends, and some of the great figures in campus journalism. I did not feel that they were models of Christian discipleship, but it astonished me to hear them talking about Christ as though they were in earnest. They are misguided, I thought, but at least they *think* they are serving God, which is a great deal more than I would have granted them before I knew them. I had not thought they would have found religion to be at all interesting. Their religious imagination, and hence their

38

argot, differed from mine, and I was not wholly successful in crediting the validity of their notions of God, since they did not speak of their experiences in my terms.

I was especially careful about terminology at this epoch. The ultimate test for all phraseology was whether or not it included this one: "Accept the Lord Jesus Christ as your personal Savior." Whatever else a person said, if he could say this, then he was on the side of the angels. But if he did not describe his experience of God thus, he had yet to discover that experience. I also liked the sound of "Christ in you," and "The blood of Jesus Christ," and "Millions are perishing," and "What doth it profit a man." I felt that these things ought to form the currency of one's conversation. I listened to ministers to see if they said the correct things. Once a man I knew used the phrase "the Christ event." I thought, "Oh, pshaw. What is this? Clearly he is not born again, or he would not be talking that way. Besides, he is from the University of Chicago Divinity School, which explains it." I did not like the idea of *the* Christ anyway. It was Jesus Christ—not even Jesus the Christ.

Some time later I was talking to some friends about "Jesus," and at the end of the conversation, an elderly man came up to me and said, "Son, give him his full title." I thought back through the conversation, trying to see what he could mean. I thought perhaps he meant that I was not showing someone the proper deference. It turned out that he wanted me to say, "The Lord Jesus Christ." Anything else sounded cavalier to him.

At about this time I began to read the works of the nineteenth-century Scottish novelist George MacDonald. They seemed to have the ring of truth about them, but they frightened me. MacDonald did not share my certainties, but he was far more rigorous in his view of holiness than I. He made me angry because I felt that he was at once far more human and far more godly than I was. His characters were people who had their feet on the ground and who had come to disturbing terms with what it means to be Christian in this world. They usually referred to God as "the Father o' Jesus Christ." Since God had existed in my mind as quite a different sort of being from Jesus Christ, I found this appellation unsettling, although I would have defended it doctrinally. But the implication seemed to be that the demands of holiness lie perilously close to humdrum daily acts. I had liked the idea of visions and prayers and intensity as the mark of my religion, and not this earthy insistence on candor and charity and honesty.

A great dread had pursued me for years before this. It was the fear that I might someday be revealed for what I really was. I feared that if what I knew to be true of myself were exhibited to my family and friends and the world, I would be destroyed. I had shuffled along, trying to offset my

guilt by acts of asceticism and devotion and earnestness. But I felt, with mortal dread, that it was all to
no avail, and that the only atoning thing for me
would be that I be exposed to my peers for what I
was. Hence I became obsessed with the idea of
candor and confession as possible ways of ransom.
I wrote letters to my neighbors and high-school
teachers, confessing lies and other sins from past
years. I searched my memory a thousand times to
find the last spectre that haunted me, but I could
not exorcise it.

I fed this dread on MacDonald. Most of his bad
characters destroyed themselves by an *appearance*
of religion. His good characters were merely human
beings who did their work and were honest.

✳

During my time at college I began to work on my
intellectual categories as I had done my devotional
categories in high school. I saw the humanistic tradition and *belles lettres* (I majored in English literature) as under the divine interdict. I had a robust
idea of the Fall. It made sense to me to attach an
intellectual fall to the moral fall of humanity. This
helped greatly to make things manageable. That
is, one need never be seriously agitated by a work
of art or literature, since, if it were unsettling, one
could always say, "Yes, but the man who produced

41

that was unsaved to begin with, and so how could he have anything to say to me?"

An American literature course was my introduction to the thought of the world. I liked the ideas of Cotton and Increase Mather, Jonathan Edwards, Anne Bradstreet, and William Bradford. But I found reading them a colossal bore. I thought Franklin a lecher and was depressed in the extreme by the deism, infidelity, and transcendentalism of Bryant, Thoreau, and Emerson. I was willing to grant the prettiness of, say, "Whither . . . far through their rosy depths dost thou pursue thy solitary way?" but I saw Bryant's ideas as insidious, and I was inclined to think that he and Emerson and the others were taking a brazen delight in undermining Christian orthodoxy. I felt that they had become cynical by having consciously rejected Christ. I scribbled angrily in my copy of Emerson where he complains of Christians dwelling "with noxious exaggeration" about the person of Jesus Christ. I hissed "God damn" through my grinding teeth. I thought this was a case of something that God *would* damn eventually, and I was anxious to be on His side.

Later, as I read Chaucer and Suckling and Donne, I thought to myself, "You see what men are really like? They become lascivious. One must be pure minded."

I studied evangelical apologetics, and I became able to extirpate Kant and Hegel and Schleiermacher and Ritschl and Feuerbach and Barth and

Brunner and Tillich. I approached ideas from a position of omniscience. I would have demurred if you had suggested this. I would have pointed out to you that there were a thousand things I did not know. I could not explain the love of God, or the origin of evil, or the length of eternity, or the date of the Second Coming. I would even have gone to the liberal length of seeing in the "days" of Genesis the possibility of great periods of time, and of rejecting flood geology. This last was a favorite straw man for my geology professor, and since I knew him to be a devout Christian, I felt it was not dangerous to believe that the strata in the Grand Canyon record, not the flood, but billions of years of prehistoric activity. I felt exhilarated by this sort of venture.

But I did feel that I was in an unassailable position philosophically. We were the recipients of the Word of God, and one of the tenets in our creed was the perspicuity of Scripture. That is, if God had communicated with us at all, He must have done so in terms that we could grasp. Scripture was not a book of sybilline hints and hieroglyphs. Its meaning is clear. Therefore, there can be no threat to one's sense of confidence. I had a vivid awareness of what it felt like to be a member of the one group in the world which was *right*. I thought about great minds, and I saw them as long since lost. I thought about Catholic theologians, and it troubled me that they could affirm all the points that I felt were vital to salvation (the Incarnation, the Virgin Birth, the Atonement, the Resurrection) and still be lost. I felt that they had not accepted the Lord Jesus Christ as their personal Savior. This was the trouble with Tillich and with Barth, too. They were arguing in a vacuum. It was no good their talking about Christ when they had not met Him. I had a hearty dislike for German idealism and other bad ideas that had made inroads into Protestant theology.

＊

In my last semester at college, I studied aesthetics under a great and good man named Kilby. We read essays by dreadful men on the theory of mimetic creation, and I began to wonder for the first time in my life just what was signaled in the whole phenomenon of art. I had, up to this point, enjoyed periodic visits to the Philadelphia Museum of Art. I had liked the seventeenth century Flemish and Dutch schools, with their clean kitchens and rutted roads and tempestuous skies, and the eighteenth century English landscapes, with their hay wagons and hedgerows. The gilded mediaeval triptychs of the Annunciation or the Crucifixion had, on the other hand, seemed a hideous misapprehension of the biblical idea. The portraits of Renaissance cardinals and dukes always looked suety to me, and I did not at all care for the acres of flesh in Rubens, or the entirely too obvious fascination of painters with the nude human form. I never knew where to look. Usually I managed a quick scrutiny as I passed en route to a suit of armor at the end of the gallery. All twentieth century painters were, of course, wicked. You could tell this simply by glancing at their distortions and dabblings and choices of subject matter. This is chaos, I thought. Picasso is a bad man to have painted the "Demoiselles d'Avignon." And what can he have been about in the "Guernica"? Horses and women and bulls simply do not look like that. Rouault was just as bad, with his heavy black outlines around everything, and the nightmarish visions of de Chirico and Delvaux and Kirchner had no business on canvas. Paul Klee's twittering birds were silly and an imposition. What Mondrian was up to I could not think. I had not yet seen Jackson Pollock or Andy Warhol.

My feelings about music had been similar. What I liked was a good melody that you could whistle. Anything post-Brahms was cacophany. Something had gone wrong, starting with Ravel, and getting worse in Bartók and Stravinsky, and deteriorating completely in the pure ugliness of Hindemith, Schoenberg, and Copland. (No one had heard John Cage yet.) There had been nothing but decline from the twin peaks of Bach and Mozart. Beethoven was an undoubted third.

All forms of dance and drama were, of course, out

45

and hence found no place in my aesthetic theories.

But then we began, in this class, to read Benedetto Croce, José Ortega y Gasset, Roger Fry, Herbert Read, Bernard Bosanquet, and I. A. Richards, and we shouted at each other and tore our hair and tried to define beauty and truth and goodness and wrote great splashy papers and looked at paintings and listened to Mozart and wondered if we would ever be able to pull ourselves together. The boy who sat next to me, who was himself an artist, leaned over one day and said that the whole thing made him feel that he was going to break out in boils. I wrote "Boo!" and "Bravissimo!" and "No, no!" and "Oyez, oyez!" in the margin of my textbook.

Questions began to arise in my mind. Was I to understand that art was not, after all, an amusing pastime? Were paintings more than wallpaper? Was the artist interested in something other than lovely vignettes? Was there something being said here about the nature of human experience? What if a man were unhappily aware of ugliness and botch in the world? Was he bad for being angry or for presenting it to us on a canvas? What demands did integrity make on an artist? Did they qualify his freedom to paint only loveliness? What constitutes sentimentalism? Was it a sin? What about the quest for form? How did this affect a man's iconography? If a painter were not concerned with photography, what *was* in his mind? What is implied in the great effort in all of poetry and music and

46

painting, to *see* and *shape* and *articulate* human experience? Is there more at stake in existence than what we busy ourselves with every day? What of the commonplace? Are we, in effect, blind? Do we fail to see terror and glory lying all about us? Is this what art is about?

I wondered. I was not sure where this kind of inquiry might lead, and uncertainty was not a frame of mind I at all welcomed at this epoch. I wanted verities. I wanted prophetic maxims with which to attack the carnality and sloth of Christendom. I did not care to entertain a whole new array of ideas that raised more questions than they answered. But I felt that once again a door had been blown open and that I could never again insist that there was nothing on the far side. I would perhaps have to begin to think of life in terms of quest rather than of arrival.

During the year after my graduation from college I traveled with a university student organization. I felt that this was God's place for me for that year, and I did my job seriously. It was the first time in my life that I had been entirely alone and free to make my own choices in the world.

Once on a vista-domed train between San Francisco and Portland, I went to the club car and suddenly ordered a blackberry cordial. It was the middle of the afternoon. I did not know what drinks belonged to what hours of the day, and this sounded good. I sat looking out at Mt. Shasta, sipping the fiery syrup and trying to capture a feeling of independence and luxury.

I spent a great deal of time in hotels in cities across the country during that year. I would walk slowly through the lobbies, looking around to see what I could see. I felt frightened and tingly, but nothing ever happened. One night in Omaha I stood at the open window of my room, gazing down at the street. I began to look at the young passers-by as bodies, and I felt out of breath. I began to imagine having someone in, but the idea of actually establishing a contact terrified me.

I was drafted into the Army at the end of that school year. There was a month's interval before my induction, so I went to visit my sister in the jungle of Ecuador. Since I had spent a summer there two years before this, I knew some of the Indians. Their names—Gervacio, Alberto, Elias, Camilo— had haunted me during the two years since I had seen them. They called me *Don* Tomas instead of Señor, which was how they usually addressed gringos. I imagined myself spending the rest of my life with them, and when the Piper Pacer lifted me away from the airstrip, back toward America and Ft. Benning, I struggled again with the sensation of irrecoverable time. I loved them, and they loved me.

Now time would pass, and they would go on with their lives and I with mine, and if we ever saw each other again there would be no way of erasing the interval. I would be older and so would they, and it would have been a ghastly cheat. Time keeps flipping the pages, even the pages on which there is a picture of Eden.

During the week before I took my toothbrush and razor to Local Board #6 in Mount Holly to join the other men on the bus to Newark, where we were to be sworn into the Army, I read *Crime and Punishment* and listened again and again to the "Overture to William Tell." There is a plaintive oboe section before the famous Lone Ranger burst, and those bars will forever sound like a knell to me. Another world had come to an end. The sergeants in the Army were not going to be impressed with my achievements, much less with my convictions and visions.

On the bus going to Newark I sat alone. Across the aisle sat another boy, also alone. He wore clear-rimmed glasses and looked as though he might have gone to college. He had a bemused look on his face, and I thought that if I could get to know him, I might survive. Two seats in front of me sat another civilized-looking boy, smiling and chatting to anyone who would listen. It did not seem to matter to him that his neighbors had long greasy hair, bad teeth, dirty jeans, or were smoking. He chatted on, joking with them about our common doom.

We were unloaded at a warehouse in Newark. I sat on a metal folding chair and relinquished all thought of sanity, much less of joy, forever. I kept hearing people around me intoning, "You better give your soul to God, 'cause the Army's got your ass," and I hated them for being able to see anything at all funny in the situation. I was disgusted by the scatological and genital fixation of everyone's conversation. Women were referred to as "broads," or by a four-letter synecdoche. Men were seen as having one function in life. I thought I could not stand hearing once more the three- and four-syllable epithets conferring perversion and incest on everyone.

That evening I sat in a room at Ft. Dix and looked out of a window next to me. I saw officers' cars going past, on their way home, and for the first time in my life I valued liberty. I was not free to rise from my chair, much less to leave the room or the area or the post. It was only a matter of a few feet, or a few hundred yards, but things had occurred (I was male, I was twenty-two, America had a policy of conscription, here was a sergeant) that established an abyss between what I was inclined to do and what I was permitted to do. I looked out at the grass and at the asphalt, and thought of the feet of the people who were free to come and go along there while I must sit in my chair. It all seemed like a gigantic mummery to me, and I could not convince myself that it was real. This is a farce, I thought. What possible right has this man, who has never heard of me and will never see me again, to say anything at all to me? I should like to get up now and go down that street. Does he actually have the power to forbid it?

I made a success of basic training at Ft. Benning. It was partly through fear of displeasing someone and partly because I was thin and did not mind drilling and running and calisthenics. They gave me a blue felt band with sergeant's stripes on it to wear on the sleeve of my fatigues. I had to drill the platoon sometimes, and take charge of the barracks. I barked "Tansh-HUT!" and "Right HOO!" and "Hut-hawp-hut-hawp-hut-hore-yer-left-right-HOO!" I began to enjoy barracks life and felt very emancipated that, when during the final weeks of training men were allowed passes into Columbus and came back drunk, I could take a tolerant view of it all. I began to feel that a person could accept as friends the men who came in drunk, without clucking at them every time, even though he might take a poor view of drunkenness.

I was reassigned to Ft. Benning as a chaplain's assistant after my training. This had nothing to do with whether or not a person was religious. The Army needed typists, and I was glad to have the job. It gave me a private office, a large desk, armchair, telephone, bookcase, and, above all, an air conditioner. Not even the colonel of the battle group had this. He had to get along with a fan.

This was the first period in my life in which I was forced to find my friends among people from backgrounds that differed radically from mine. Basic training and barracks life had had a limbering effect on my frame of mind, however, and I began to experience a certain curiosity and zest in discovering new kinds of people.

A contest arose between me and some of the cadre, especially the First Sergeant and the Sergeant Major, who took the view that a chaplain's assistant was by definition a military loss. I amused myself by showing them that I could be as Prussian as they. I eventually got them onto my side, and the First Sergeant used to mutter at me as we passed each other, "Hey, Howard, say a prayer for old Rangel."

I found life endlessly diverting. I got on well, for example, with several old lechers and alcoholics from the Motor Pool. I thought back to the days in boarding school when I resented having anyone sit on the edge of my bed for fear of mess and germs. And those boys were Christians. Now I could lie on my bunk and watch an old sergeant sit down next to me, drink from a bottle of vodka, then pour what was left onto the floor and light it.

One day in the chapel I heard the sounds of J. S. Bach coming from the organ in the choir loft and went up to see who else in the United States Army liked Bach. It was a master sergeant, and he and his wife and I became fast friends. We had a recorder trio, and used to meet in the evenings and play Telemann and Corelli and Orlando Gibbons. I met a cook, a young Dutch immigrant, in our company mess, who turned out to be a Bach worshiper also, and we would storm about his living room conducting the "Goldberg Variations" and "Wachet Auf, Ruft Uns die Stimme," with great flourish.

Once I walked into my office and heard arias from "Cosi Fan Tutte" and "Pagliacci" coming from the chapel auditorium. I went in and discovered a recruit flinging himself about, performing entire operatic scenes in a deafening falsetto. He had escaped from K.P. He turned out to be a Jewish boy named Hickins who had lived all over Europe and who seemed to speak half the languages of the world. I saw in him a cultivated finesse and flair that attracted me.

An Italian boy appeared in my door one day and asked, after some tentative stammering, if there were any sort of Bible study going. I happened to have organized one, and he began to come frequently. He was a poet and musician, and we had long conversations about Paradise and beauty and passion and music and how intolerable everything was.

My Dutch friend called me to the mess hall one day, telling me that there was a recruit on K.P. I had to meet. He turned out to be English, and the most urbane and literate person I had ever met. We took long walks together, and read poetry, and argued theism. I later recognized him as the soldier who had laughed one day as I passed him on my bicycle. I asked him why he had done that, and he said it was from sheer delight at seeing someone on a bike again. He hadn't known Americans rode bicycles. I liked his hard mind and his blasé knowledge of the world and things; and I tried to pick up what I could from his conversation without letting him know I was wholly naïve.

I wrote an article in the Ft. Benning newspaper, arguing that the two years in the Army need not be a total waste of time for the draftees (as opposed to the enlistees, who had chosen it, and hence ought not to be subject to the same feeling of frustration). My article was assailed in the following issue by a person named Weinraub. I spotted a soldier in the mess hall one day who I thought might be he, and sat down. We began to parry a bit, and an amusing friendship started. I liked his dry, low-pressure, slightly amused and unsentimental approach to things. I tried to learn from him not to be so earnest.

I had a great deal of time to myself and began to read. I mapped out my study time, allotting time for the Bible, the Greek New Testament, philosophy, and novels. I began to read the Gospels and make notes, trying to dissociate my imagination from every possible notion that I had had about them. I tried not to read into the description of Jesus what was not there, but to approach it from a standpoint of curiosity rather than knowledge. It was not easy, but Jesus began to emerge as much less ethereal and much more human than I had thought Him to be.

I read Bertrand Russell's *History of Western Philosophy*. I liked being able to talk about Thales and Duns Scotus and Bergson and logical positivism. Russell's breezy boldness amused me. I drew diagrams of Kant's theories of knowledge.

Lady Chatterley's Lover appeared while I was at Ft. Benning, and I bought a copy for six dollars. I was electrified by the famous passages. I had never seen such things on a printed page before. I read them and reread them, aghast. After I became able to read the whole story with some equanimity, I began to wonder if Lawrence was, after all, a bad man. Clearly, he was in earnest. I found his images of impotence and sterility and passion compelling. I wondered if there were anything in his idea of "tenderness and sensuality." Some time later I argued with a man who took a poor view of the whole thing, and I defended Lawrence as someone who saw.in human sexuality a significance almost sacramental. I felt at that moment that I was letting my literary theories run ahead of my moral categories, but I found the exercise exhilarating.

When the day came for my separation from active duty (the Army did not use the term "discharge" in those days), I discovered a hint of nostalgia. Somehow the yellow wooden buildings and the sand and Australian pines and the shimmering heat of the Georgia summers and the plodding sameness of Ft. Benning life took on a different color in retrospect. I felt a curious affection for it all. I felt that my vision of what life was like had undergone an undefined transfiguration during the two apparently dull years. I could not assess it, but it obviously had something to do with the effect on my consciousness of the people I had lived with, especially of the five or six friends whom I had come to love. I had discovered joy in the knowledge of people whom I would have excluded from my circle at an earlier era as being of interest to me only as potential converts to my way of thinking. I thought that perhaps I ought to feel guilty and that I should try to forget them. But friendship is difficult to gainsay.

Part 2

I took a position in Philadelphia when I left the Army. I lived in the suburbs with my parents and decorated my room in a way that worried everyone. I painted one wall slate gray and hung up Picasso, Mondrian, Braque, Dufy, and van Ruysdael prints. I subscribed to *The Manchester Guardian, The New Statesman, The New Republic,* and *The Reporter*. I sent away for great packages of books and bought tickets to see José Greco, the Ballet Africain (no tops), and Marcel Marceau. I took the bus to New York on Friday nights and crawled around Mac-Dougall Street with a friend, looking at this demi-monde and feeling that I would like to enter it.

One thing worried me. I was sleeping until break-fast now, rather than allowing an hour for my devotions. I felt, therefore, that my life was a hollow mockery. I felt that it was not possible to grow spiritually without these exercises in private. The analogy between food for the body and the Bible for the soul possessed my imagination, and I felt that I was probably starving myself.

I was, nonetheless, unimpeachably orthodox in my creed. I looked upon myself as an incorrigible traditionalist doctrinally. I did not discover, as most of my contemporaries did, that because of the undoubted obscurantism of half the religious world and because of the excitement generated by discoveries in the physical sciences, I was able to affirm only a shorter and shorter list of things about the supernatural world. The normal pattern, in which one drops off first Jonah, then the Red Sea, then Jericho and Samson, then the feeding of the five thousand, and finally the Virgin Birth and the Resurrection and God himself, did not strike me as being entirely inevitable. This anti-faith seemed to me to spring from a hopeful trust in a set of propositions fully as perilous as anything that religious orthodoxy had ever demanded.

But I felt that I was in a limbo, with, on the one hand, a familiar world of orthodoxy in which I could no longer breathe, and, on the other, "the world," which posed a threat to my purity and my pursuit of authenticity.

I sat at my desk in the office and looked out over the smokestacks and water tanks and roof-top billboards and down to the drugstores and parking lots, and I began to fill up yellow memo slips with questions about desire and art and dogma and holiness. I wrote long and carefully articulated questions about my presuppositions and about popular additions to doctrine. Sometimes the jottings were brief. I wrote on one piece of paper, "*Is* there balm in Gilead?" and on another, "Damn," and on another "Let me implore the Church to begin some serious thinking on. . . ."

I bought avant-garde clothes at posh shops and walked blocks out of my way at lunch time in order to get down into the interesting part of the city. I hated the formica and steel and leatherette lunch counters near my office. I stood by the Wanamaker eagle, where the whole city meets, looking at the well-dressed passers-by, and picking out the ones I felt I would like to talk to. I took a room on a picturesque street near Rittenhouse Square during the winter for several weeks and walked the streets at night wondering how a person was expected to survive. I felt rhapsodically lonely and frantic for new and intoxicating experiences. I began to feel that I had wasted a decade in the pursuit of a chimerical holiness that had robbed me of the varieties of knowledge that adolescence and young adulthood seek. I was prepared to set God aside now, if to pursue Him meant to miss the cakes and ale. I saw people in this neighborhood who were obviously finding what they wanted in life, with their little Queen Anne Houses on cobbled, tree-lined streets and their MG's and brunches and parties and travel. I went to off-beat theater productions and concerts and art shows and thought "Good God. I'm on the outside."

I had several English friends in Philadelphia, and through them I secured a teaching position at a boys' school in England.

At the end of the year I sailed on an alarming old German ship, bound for Le Havre. I planned to read Fraser's enormous *Golden Bough* on board, but instead spent the whole time talking to people over beer and kirsch. I achieved a minor celebrity by performing in an amateur talent show, and I felt very worldly and international.

✳

My room at the school was about as big as a large linen closet, and I was able to keep out the gelid English weather by having the electric fire on all day. The English people object to low temperatures indoors as vigorously as Americans do, but there is a national hostility to the notion of central heating, so I had to create my own tropical enclave.

We all spent the winter with chilblains and catarrh (I had never heard of catarrh before). The boys, who rarely got near a fire at all, went about in short pants and mufflers. Their hands turned the color of raspberry mousse, and if you pressed your finger on the back of a boy's hand, you left a custard-colored blotch. I filled a "hotty" with boiling water every night and took it to bed with me.

Sometimes on a cold afternoon when I would sit alone in my room with my tea, or late at night when the housemaster would drop by for coffee, I was able to take a eupeptic view of the world. Life seemed manageable once more. I was three thousand miles from Philadelphia, whose salons had seemed shut against my quest for bliss. The days passed in a pattern, and for all the hugger-mugger of English school life, there was always the tranquillity of the long evenings after the boys were in bed.

I was enchanted with the country, and even with the weather. We were on the Irish Sea, and when it was not drizzling, there was a tempest. Months pass with no evidence at all that there is so much as a sun left in the sky. I used to groan for the English who sit on wet sand in heavy tweeds and call it a day at the beach, or spread out their pork pies, sausage rolls, and jam tarts in their Austins because there is a downpour soaking the moor outside.

The boys' vocabulary amused me. One boy wrote an essay about a sausage sizzle in the back garden. I interpreted this to mean a wiener roast in the back yard. Another came to me one evening during prep (study hours) and complained that his French assignment was "dead awkward." Another said to me one day, "Sir, was that you I saw in that whacking great armchair?" I had a sweat shirt that I wore for games. It had a large portrait of Bach on the front of it. One boy ran up to me the first time I appeared with it and said, "*Sir!* There's a parson on your tummy!" Another, looking on, said to a friend, "Dig the gaffer."

I spent some holidays with a friend in North Wales, where he lived with his two aunts in a stone cottage on the moor. We walked through an old gray wooden gate at the edge of the village and out onto the hills covered with bracken and gorse, or sat by the fire drinking Cadbury's chocolate and roasting nuts. One frosty Christmas Eve we walked through the village to Midnight Mass. There were stars, snow, cottages, the ancient church, and the silence, broken only by the bell and the occasional baa of a sheep. You felt that you ought to be bringing a lamb or frankincense.

I sometimes felt that given the right circumstances I could organize an idyll for myself. Perhaps the great thing was to fly from complexity and the possibility of chaos. I spent a great deal of time dreaming of myself walking hand in hand with someone I loved down country lanes or sitting in hushed bliss over candles and silver.

I usually went to London for my holidays and stayed with a friend at his successive flats in Bloomsbury, Hampstead, Mayfair, and Earls Court. I was glad not to be a tourist. I loved the black cabs with their smoky glass and brown leather seats. We ate in the *trattorias* of Soho, and I began to learn the names of wines.

I watched my friend with the waiters and maîtres d'hôtel. He had neither the fear that I had always known, nor the swagger of the churlish rich. He was unaffected, articulate, and pleasant with them. We went to exciting clubs where he would order elaborate cocktails, and watched brilliant satiric revues on British politics and society. Once we had dinner with an enormously wealthy *grande dame* at her apartment in Manchester Square. She swept in from the tub in a pleated coral dressing gown and waved us to the liquor cabinet. She talked rapidly on every possible topic. She was either amused or bored by everyone. I felt that these were useful categories. After dinner she laid her wrists on the edge of the table, straightened up, and said, "Well. That was damned good." I liked this sort of panache.

Once we arranged to meet a handsome socialite for a matinee. She and I arrived at the theater early and sat talking. When my friend appeared, she greeted him with "We've been sitting here talking about how awful everything is." I tried to identify this frame of mind. Having read about the same kind of thing in Evelyn Waugh and Rose Macaulay, I thought that it would be nice to have this dry, ready, jaded knowledge of the world, to be beyond being surprised or disconcerted or embarrassed, to be frank and articulate and blasé.

I had a friend who lived in the Cathedral Close

in Norwich, and I spent several holidays sailing with him on the Norfolk Broads and going with him on his visits to the crumbling Saxon, Norman, and Gothic parish churches in Norfolk. He was the architect who assessed the cost of repairs for the diocese. He worried me because he loved God and life at the same time. It had always been one or the other for me. When I had tried to pursue God, I had fled from life. When life began to be dazzling, I had let God slip. I would have called his voluptuous zest for life pagan except that it was not only matched by his appetite for God: it was part of it. He loved heraldry and John Donne and St. Benedict and four-centered arches and beer and the Mass and bodies and Bach with none of the usual timidity brought to these things by religious people. I had felt that there was a point at which joy becomes indecorous and that religious categories asked that one not become too enthusiastic about anything short of God, whom I understood to be a spirit. I was jarred to discover that my friend had no dichotomy in his mind between spiritual things and other things. One was to love the world and experience because God did and because one loved God. How else is one to express joy and worship but in merriment and affirmation? Joy was important in his creed. He was not a bacchant, however. He was not trying to attach a divine validity to mere license. He had a rigorous idea of goodness, but it did not seem to be *fragile* as mine did. It did not make him go tiptoe through life. He saw no reason to be parsimonious about joy. He was not, on the other hand, merely merry. One of his favorite expressions was "bloody hell." He would often thrust out his jaw and frown into space in perplexity over existence. All I could get from him at these moments would be "Chaos!"

We went together sometimes to St. George's Tombland, a tiny church just outside the Close. Here I saw for the first time in my life a cope and biretta and monstrance, and heard the Angelus. I was sure it was all wrong, but at least it was not Roman, and the sermons were unexceptionable. I was not prepared to write it off. There seemed to be a difference, not in dogma, but in vision, between my religious categories and this. There was a way of reading the world that was prior to one's response to dogma. If you saw a continuum of significance in all things, from the lowest worm to the highest seraph, and if you saw reality as both concealed and revealed in the observable phenomena of the world, then you were likely to understand the In- carnation as a massive attestation of the whole sacramental principle. If, on the other hand, the idea of the Fall as intervening definitively between the Creation and the rest of history, and of the post-symbolic nature of the New Testament, were the operative ideas in your consciousness, then you were likely to seek religious exercises that were minimally sensuous.

I sometimes went to Paris by myself. I thought

that this might be the place to enact the solitary gloom described by Camus, Baldwin, or Sartre. I sat in the Café de Flore in Saint-Germain-des-Prés drinking *café filtre* and trying to write great things. I felt constipated. I thought that if I were ever to write something telling, this would be the place to do it, but it all turned out to be very bathetic. I stayed in a hotel in the Rue Dragon and disliked having to ring for the concierge when I came in after two o'clock.

Sometimes I sat in the Louvre looking at the Venus, or at the Nike of Samothrace. I felt that my view of man-made beauty had been an inadequate one. I had been able to simplify things by eliminating practically everything. In so far as I was able to see a thing as under the divine interdict, I was safe from it. Praxiteles and Michelangelo and Epstein were great and accomplished men, but they had nothing, really, to tell me. Most sculpture sprang from the worship, either of pagan gods or of the human form, and for me, the one area was wholly evil, and the other was highly dangerous. The contemplation of art was an activity likely to lead one into idolatry, and I feared this. It is easy enough to see the fatuousness and preciosity of people who make a career of appreciating art, and I wanted to escape that sort of thing. But the sheer power of beauty troubled me. How could I dismiss as mere idolatry something that was perfect?

The more I traveled around the Continent, the more I experienced a conflict of sensibility. There was one part of me that liked stone cottages and fireside teas and tranquillity and simplicity and familiar religious practices. But, on the other hand, I became less and less sure that I wanted a walled-in euphoria. If a wide range of experience meant chaos and hurly-burly and pain, it also meant knowledge. And who can opt for ignorance? It is easy enough to be content if you exclude nearly everything from your consciousness. But this is not an authentic foundation for contentment. The great thing, I felt, would be to discover everything, and *then* make my choices. It was the difference between innocence and goodness. The man whose righteousness is untested is not undoubtedly righteous. If strawberries were evil, and I detested strawberries, or had never seen one, I would not be able to claim sainthood in a world where strawberries were the test of one's powers of voluntary abstinence. The only way anyone would know whether or not I was, in fact, a truly good man would be if I had seen strawberries, known them to be irresistibly delicious, and had renounced them in the name of moral categories which excluded them. It would be no good to act as though there were none or that I did not want them.

I saw the hungry curiosity on the faces of the passers-by along the Boulevard St. Michel and in the Deux Magots and Le Fiacre, and I contrasted this with the clear-eyed confidence on the faces of people I had known, and I was far from sure that I preferred the latter. Babies in the womb are at peace, and people who think they are in the womb are at peace, but it is a peace achieved at the expense of actuality. I did not want this.

*

I began to suspect, however, that this scuffle in my sensibilities between the fireside and the boulevard signaled another, more elementary conflict. There was clearly a bitter debate occurring between some remorseless inquisitor who called all my efforts at fulfillment into the dock, and another figure who sought energetically to justify my inclinations. It was a debate between the anchorite and the sybarite.

I had encountered a world that burst the seams of my ideas about life. I began, therefore, to examine my whole understanding of religious and moral dogma. The question posed by the serpent in the story of Eden ("Hath God said?") was the great question. If you hold a set of notions that imposes strictures on your inclinations, you begin to look for ways of circumventing the strictures without incurring guilt. It would be helpful, for instance, if you could discover that your ideas had suddenly become archaic or that new light had opened up new possibilities of interpretation on these absolutes.

What began as a struggle between the moral absolutism of dogmatic orthodoxy on the one hand

and the appeal of what is commonly called freedom on the other, eventually grew into a full-dress criticism, carried on by myself, of the whole nature and shape of my own religious sensibilities.

Obviously a shift had occurred in these sensibilities. I found that the entire set of desiderata to which the religious appeal is commonly addressed had evaporated for me. That is, I no longer shared the *frame of mind* that ordinarily marks the religious approach to life.

For one thing, I was not in the least anxious to belong to any sort of cognoscenti or illuminati. I had encountered a dozen forms of this as an outsider, and it had not been an attractive thing. I had sat in meetings during my undergraduate days and listened to men thanking God that they and they alone held the truth. It seemed to me that, even if this were the case, this was hardly the posture. They and their wives had walked past me for three years with glassy stares of unfamiliarity, and I had watched other new arrivals who were known to be "of them" welcomed with open arms. I felt petulant. I had felt like saying, well, a pox, then. I had also encountered groups whose mark seemed to be a secretive earnestness, a delighted desire that I, too, enter into the richness which they enjoyed. I felt that they used kindness and enthusiasm and smiles as ways of helping me into the light. Everyone seemed to have found the key to it all and to be delighted at the prospect of another initiate.

But what put me off about these people had undoubtedly been experienced by others visiting my own group. Once, when I was a boy, a woman from another religion had come over to our side. She was a tall, thin, intelligent person who belonged to one of Philadelphia's first families. We crowded around her and said, "Praise the Lord." I remember her smiling and stammering, "Yes, I guess that's it." We soon frightened her off. I heard later that she had "absolutely reneged." I felt that she was guilty of perfidy.

Half of the world, I knew, mentioned this sort of thing as the reason for their disaffection from religion. They could not tolerate hypocrisy and cant. But this seemed to me to be throwing out the baby with the bath. In so far as one feels anything at all to be true, and feels himself to be the recipient of that truth, he can be said to belong to a cognoscenti. It may be the Americans for Democratic Action or the Coptic Church. All of us think we see things more clearly than our fellows do. But I dreaded the frame of mind that results when this notion is given a divine validity. I was not against the idea of truth. I was against anything that appeared as unctuousness and stridence and complacency.

I found, too, that I disliked the shape that popular religion has taken in our century, especially the confusion of that shape with religion itself. For better or worse, in the tradition with which I was familiar, the business of being godly is associated with various social images, and these images frightened me. I wanted to find out what it would be like for a man to love God and not 1) live in a ranch house, 2) drive a station wagon, 3) marry, 4) find his friends among bright young couples, 5) commute, 6) go to bed at ten o'clock, 7) eat three specified meals a day. Why, I wondered, are there some images that make everyone feel safe and others that put us on edge? How do they become confused with religion? What if you wanted to wear bell-bottomed trousers and a beard? Would everyone still feel comfortable about your *morals*? They might deplore your taste, but would they read a moral significance into your appearance? This was the thing that disturbed me. I did not see that the tests for goodness lay in appearance. I could not see that the young salesman with his fedora, attaché case, and gray suit *looked* any more godly than the bespectacled, sandaled, parti-colored teeny-bopper sitting in Washington Square.

But the fedora-attaché case image was the image that attended my wing of religion. That is, if someone looked like that, we felt that he was on the right road (given, of course, some spiritual qualifications). If, on the other hand, a person with exactly the same spiritual qualifications chose to live in a mews loft and sit behind dark glasses drinking espresso until 4 A.M., we would have been concerned. We would have felt that he needed to be put on the right track. We established a continuum in our imaginations between what a person *looked* like and what he *was*.

This sort of imagination operates in two directions. From the inside of a given milieu a person looks around to find out whether people look as though they might fit comfortably in with him. From the outside, others look in and build up archetypes in their minds as to what he and his friends look like. I had often done it. I had thought, for instance, of the archetypal Episcopalian as being a gloved, blue-haired dowager with steel-rimmed pince-nez. My Presbyterian image was of bright, liberal, engagé seminarians, and adroit ecclesiastical politicians. Pentecostalism suggested shouting, ropy-necked women with knotted hair, and the Baptists seemed to have a great many fat and sweating preachers.

I was not yet able to disentangle goodness from what my imagination told me good people looked like, and since these people looked like nothing I ever wanted to be, I was prepared to scotch the notion of goodness.

Another thing that worried me about the shape of popular religion was the array of devout exercises that was seen by each group as having a unique and a divine validity. That is, people who were loyalists of *any* form of religious orthodoxy assumed that their set of gestures, and their set alone, represented true love for God.

Our gestures are determined, of course, by our

understanding of what true devotion involves. I do not know what the differences in exercise are between nominal and zealous Hindus, for instance, I know some of the varieties of scruple among Jews. Among Christians the variety is infinite. Some disavow any visible devotion at all, arguing that the religion of Christ is not to be found in any hallowed enclaves of worship. Jesus as the Man for Others, rather than Jesus Christ the Rex Gloriae, is central in their imagining. Others buy an outfit at Bergdorf and appear at St. Thomas's Church on Easter morning and thereby discharge their duty to God and Fifth Avenue. Some play the organ for half a century in Cedar Rapids without missing a Sunday, launder the altar linen, give out tracts, or attend daily Mass or weekly prayer meeting. The devotional equipment may be a rosary or an annotated Bible. The great thing is to discover some activity that signals good intentions before God. The trouble with human imagination is that it would like very much to transform whatever the activity is into merit, so that some automatic efficacy attaches to it. We resist this suggestion vigorously if someone calls our attention to it, but there is almost no way of keeping ourselves free from the inclination to magic. We like to see others' gestures as vain, idolatrous, or superstitious, but it does not often occur to us to think about what would be left of our own righteousness if the familiar equipment were suddenly to vanish.

In my wing of Christendom, for instance, it was

common enough to point out the alchemy that attends Catholic Christianity. It looked to us as though these people had succeeded in shifting the focus from an inner, dynamic holiness to a set of exercises that would guarantee things for them. The lighting of candles before images, crossing oneself, genuflecting, the use of holy water, compulsory attendance at Mass—it all looked like an attempt to win the benefits of righteousness without meeting the rigorous demands made upon the inner man by Christ. It did not occur to us that their rejoinder to our criticisms would have been the same as ours to their comments about *our* exercises: these things represent only outward tokens of an inner energy. We would have said to them, "Yes, but the breakdown here is that, whether or no, the tokens begin to replace the energy in the human imagination, so that the question becomes not, 'Have I *prayed*?' but rather, 'Have I said my beads?' and not, 'Have I actually said to *God*, "Asperges me," ' but, 'Did a drop of holy water fall on me?' "

It is easy enough to point out this kind of thing in sacramentalism. But it is a more subtle affair in a kind of religion whose proud mark is that it claims to insist on inner purity. The great effort of the Reformation was to reassert what it felt to be the Biblical focus on the heart, and to simplify and dramatize the pursuit of goodness by stripping away the equipment that tended to lead men's imaginations away from the radicals. So that Protestants resist having you point out their talismans to them.

Nonetheless, religious exercises in our sector involved several things. The most obvious to the outsider would have been the focus on meetings. One was committed to a rapid succession of meetings. This was the principal exercise of the faithful. Your devotion was measured in direct ratio to the number of times you appeared at gatherings in the course of one week. There were a thousand types of gathering, and each one had an unexceptionable urgency and an unanswerable rationale behind it. If you loved God, you did not "forsake the assembling of yourselves together as the manner of some is." This meant Sunday morning. If you really loved Him, you were eager to come again that evening. If you were dead serious, you assisted during the afternoon at public meetings on the street or at groups for young people. It was not to be questioned that you understood prayer to mean Wednesday night in the church. Nor was it in doubt that you were interested enough in your religion to join in special Bible study groups on another evening. And your loyalty to the group would express itself further by your helping at the supper on Friday night and at the church officers' meeting on another night. Saturday night was the big night on the town when all Christians appeared at "rallies"—large efforts to attract converts attended by music, fun, and preaching.

The weekly pattern was not the only thing. You spent your holiday at a Christ-centered resort. This meant that the other people there shared your views. It safeguarded you from having to mix with uncongenial types. There was an atmosphere of fun and familiarity. There were likely to be daily meetings. There were attractive rustic signs nailed to the pine trees quoting selections from the Bible. Once in the souvenir shop at one of these places I bought a small hand game involving a ball and cup. On the handle was printed, "Let every man be swift to hear, slow to speak, slow to wrath." I took this to be a warning, well placed in my case, against losing your temper over your failure to get the ball into the cup. You could buy pencils and wall plaques with similar injunctions.

These resorts varied in character, from the speed-boat-dungarees-hullaballoo sort of thing, where the religion was marked by an image of breathless virility, to decorous retreats where the women went about in white oxfords with soft cardigans thrown around their shoulders (never on). The equipment at both places was likely to be a thumbed Bible, a pencil, and a small snap-ring notebook. There always seemed to be women who had lived in India, and who stood about in small groups chatting quietly. My impression was one of hot sand, pine needles, screen doors, and silence.

There were celebrities in this world, as there are in any. At the new centers the heroes were often sports figures who had become Christian, or speakers who wore Hawaii shirts and dental cream smiles, and who could make the house rock with laughter at one moment, and shudder over the awareness of hell at the next. At the older places the dignitaries were often English and could expound passages from the Bible for long periods of time, drawing rococo analogies from every phrase in the Old and New Testaments. I listened to one man discover a pattern for the whole of morality and eschatology in this sentence: "And Saul tarried in the uttermost part of Gibeah under a pomegranate tree." Another man found forty minutes' worth of spiritual admonition in this: "Crescens to Galatia." I was not sure that I even grasped the syntax of the text, but we went from the meeting feeling that we had been blessed.

I went back to one of these conferences after several years' absence, and found that the iteration from the pulpit of things that everyone was fully aware of was the thing that aroused the gasps of admiration and nods of accord. People seemed to enjoy hearing affirmed what they already vigorously believed and to find in this activity what they called "a real blessing." It reminded me of these small wheel-shaped cages in which a squirrel can run madly for as long as he likes without covering any territory.

The thing that frightened me about all this was not the earnestness and devotion. I admired this, as I admired the Lady Julian of Norwich or David Livingston or St. John of the Cross. It was the assumption that this was what religion looked like. Love for God became visible in worn-out Bibles and familiar argot and frequent gathering. The focus did not seem to have anything particular to do with the things Christ insisted on. You busied yourself with the appointed exercises, and the further you were able to banish other areas of human experience from your attention, the better. The great thing was to feel pure before God. This purity was reached, not by pedestrian choices but by devotional activities.

This whole vision seemed to me to involve an effort to escape existence and to find a *refuge* in religion. It was an effort that no longer appealed to me. I had lost, somewhere, any desire to find in religion a buffer between myself and existence. This is a trying thing to discover if you are at the same time anxious to discover God, in that the religious appeal is commonly addressed to your assumed desire to find a refuge. But what if that is the last thing you want? A refuge from what? Usually the appeal takes a highly metaphorical form, involving seas, gales, shoals, thunder, and a small bark. What was one to understand by this picture, I wondered. What, exactly, *is* the tumult? The morning rush hour? Politics? The professional scramble? High speed automobiles? Responsibility? Horrid people? Bad news? Whatever it was, it seemed to me that the desire to escape it all was a natural, but not a religious, desire.

The difficulty with this is that, for whatever reasons, there is a whole generation now that wants anything but tranquillity. Its worst fears are of trammels and ennui. George Fox's invitation to "Come out of the bustlings, you that are bustling," may have sounded like an invitation to paradise to his generation, but to a generation marked by the frug and cafés-a-go-go and swingers and trans-atlantic travel and happenings and high camp and discotheques and Carnaby Street and beach houses, it sounds like an invitation to the tundra. The great thing is to discover all of experience—the fun and games, the passion and heartbreak, and the chaos, despair and ecstasy.

I found that I shared this sensibility. I was aware that tranquillity is available from various sources (Zen, barbiturates, cretinism, religion), and it was not this that I sought. I wanted above anything else to *know*, and if the world was a tempest, then I wanted to be in it and not in a backwater. If integrity and courage asked that one not be exempted from the actualities of existence, then I could not see as legitimate a peace achieved by opting into a haven. It will be objected, of course, that true religion does not bring us euphoria, and that, far from letting us out of the hurly-burly, it asks that we face things, but face them in a new light. I would have admitted this. It was simply that, to my mind, religious faith ordinarily seemed to crowd one into a sort of corral, and I wanted to be free to caper across the downs.

I sometimes wanted to drive madly through the streets in a troika like Dmitri Karamazov, flogging the horses into a bloody lather, or to fling, black-browed and gnashing like Heathcliff, across the moor under raggedy clouds, or to sit, spectre-like, at a table in Saint-Germain, brooding over coffee and cigarettes. If this was what life held for the person who wanted to find it all out, then this was what I wanted. The imagery appealed to me far more than cardigans and pine needles.

To my mind, the great thing was a heightened consciousness, and I saw experience as the vehicle of this consciousness. To be authentically human meant to be awake and curious and passionate and questing, never satisfied with things as they appear, forever trying to break up the glaze that coats things. It meant, above all, to be free.

I had, of course, a special idea as to what freedom implied. It was not an uncommon one. When you talk about freedom to this age, people understand you to mean travel and people and sex and orgies and LSD and marijuana and music and smoke and the liberty to come and go without ulterior considerations.

The difficulty that this mind has with religion is that religion seems to busy itself with imposing strictures on experience. Surely the rigor and committal it asks of one is a gaunt thing. Surely the narrowing down of focus implies a lowering of consciousness and vitality. The world is full of an enormous variety of experiences, and they all must contribute to the process of one's becoming fully human. That is, in so far as there is a given experience, especially a pleasure, to be had, one abstains from it to one's own impoverishment.

Take, as an analogy, the relationship of music and pleasure. A person born totally deaf has no problem, presumably, with what he is missing. The fact that he cannot hear, say, the "Recordare, Jesu Pie," from Mozart's *Requiem,* or hear Leontyne Price sing "Ch'il bel sogno," does not arouse intense anguish. But a man who has heard this music has a different problem. Suppose he had come to love it and to find in it a great joy. Then suppose one of two things happened. Let us say he lost his hearing. He would have to come to terms with the loss of a known pleasure. Depending on his fortitude and sensitivity, he could either accept the tragedy with equanimity, or he could kick and scream. On the other hand, let us say that he learned suddenly that music was interdicted. He would have an entirely different problem. He would say to himself, "There is Mozart. And I have a set of ears. The combination of these two brings me sublime pleasure, even rapture. Indeed, I find the Beatific Vision itself adumbrated in the experience. And now I am told that it is forbidden. Am I to understand that, odd as it may seem, *listening* to Mozart (as opposed to the music itself, which is neutral) has some deleterious effect on me?"

The analogy suggests this, I think: we feel that inasmuch as there is a dimension of experience

81

present in the world, we are the larger for having encountered it. Otherwise travel, music, gourmet cooking, sex, poetry, and painting would have no appeal for us. We feel that these things contribute to an enlarging of our consciousness, and may, therefore, be sought. But then we run afoul of strictures which circumscribe our quest for what we see to be fulfillment, and we boggle. Religion looked to me suspiciously like an attempt to make us deaf, or, if our ears are good, to torment us with interdicts.

It seemed to me that frequently the popular imagination of what it meant to have found a refuge in Christ came close to a back-to-the-womb syndrome. A baby is secure, warm, and satisfied. If given his choice, he would stay there forever. He can neither imagine nor desire what is outside. If you told him how nice it is to have friends, and how good artichokes and moselle are, he would recoil in fear and disgust. The security that my religious friends enjoyed appeared to me in this light. Of course they feel secure, I thought. They have opted out of most of what makes the world exciting and risky.

*

The vision of religion as a haven involves, then, an exclusion of various areas of experience from one's attention. Associated with this there comes an effort to safeguard the religious structure by giving these exclusions a moral validity. That is, in so far as you can call what you exclude bad, it is easier to manage. You find that, in order to protect your ideas, the easiest thing is to build walls and call what lies outside bad.

This results in what we call taboo. All systems of dogmatic orthodoxy are marked by taboo. It is in the nature of the case, and it is not necessarily to be deprecated. Obviously, if you think something is good, you thereby think something else is bad. If you belong to the Anti-Defamation League of B'nai Brith, you see certain attitudes as sub-human and uncivilized, and you put money and energy into stamping out what you do not like. If you belong to the Black Muslims, you have a set of goals before you, and you see this and that and the other thing as obstacles and threats, and you attack them. If you are a good Marxist, you will not buy into stocks or real estate. If you are a vegetarian, you will not want to prepare a roast.

The trouble with my own crowd, in my opinion, was that, in a zealous effort to be loyal to the rigorous moral code described in the Hebrew and Christian scriptures, they had out-godded God. They understood the Sinaitic taboos to be legal figures for what later emerged as a dynamic system of human goodness that insisted first, last, and always on a purity of heart that could never be guaranteed by external scruple. We knew how Christ had excoriated the orthodox Jews for tithing mint, anise, and cummin at the same time that they ignored the very things that all the mint and cummin was about, namely justice and mercy and faith. Christ must have appeared as very naïve and worldly to his religious contemporaries, in that he spent half of his time knocking in the head their efforts to keep things pure. The trouble was that, in the attempt, they had lost the vibrancy of the whole thing. They ended up with a brittle system of morality that had nothing to do with godliness, in Christ's opinion. St. Paul, who was certainly as inclined to codify as any of us, fulminated against the unceasing effort of the Christians to get things manageable by making them visible and structured. He wrote off their lists of interdicts as of no value and as inimical to the doctrine of Christ. And yet they thought of themselves as the custodians of God's holiness. They saw the world at large romping about in a Dionysian frolic, and they thought that they could register their disaffection by marking out a few areas in which they clearly differed from their neighbors. But they were told that it would not do. This sort of thing may have a show of severity and humility, but it is merely pettifogging, said St. Paul.

The shouting irony, to my mind, was that an orthodoxy that saw itself as the heir to Christ and St. Paul was the very orthodoxy that had become famous in our century for its interdicts. If you ask someone what he thinks of when he thinks of a fundamentalist, he will probably tell you that it is a person who does not drink or smoke or gamble or go to the theater. God in heaven, I thought. This is the irony of the aeon. Here is a crowd that urges a kind of divine purity whose locale is in the heart —the *heart*—and, in the effort to safeguard and promulgate this idea, they have gutted their dogma. They have substituted a brittle and fragile and precarious structure of morals for the sinewy, resilient, vibrant sort of thing that their God insists on.

The complexities in this structure were infinite, and incomprehensible to an outsider. If the taboos had been understood as matters of taste or inclination or health, no one could argue. But they were given a divine authority.

I knew people, for instance, who, in the name of religion, had to spend time deciding between the Beatles and the Lettermen, as to which group could be listened to without sin. They did not allow music if that music had been heard on a film, and they objected to long straight hair on girls if that was the fashion of the moment and to short hair if that was the fashion. I spent some time once with another, equally earnest group, that was vigorously aware of the number of inches between the sleeve and the wrist and between the hemline and the floor. They, too, were inclined to regard hair styles as having moral significance and saw a bun as probably the most godly arrangement. Chignons and French twists did not qualify. Another group objected to earrings but not to necklaces or bracelets. Another used clear finger-nail polish but not colored, and another used lipstick but not mascara. Many, of course, objected to all make-up (powder and hand cream seemed to have been given a special indulgence).

The rationale offered was a quotation from the Bible: "Abstain from all appearance of evil" (from the same author, I recalled, who had blasted the religious effort to preserve an appearance of good by calling *things* wrong). The idea was that all sorts of bad women, from Jezebel and Cleopatra to Maria Theresa and Clara Bow, had used make-up, and if one were to avoid the appearance of evil, one did not use paints. I remember hearing one girl fling in the teeth of a less zealous girl, "I never put a thing on my face." At the time I agreed with her doctrine, but I had misgivings about her face as an example of divine loveliness.

This effort to establish a continuum between evil and *things* chilled me. It seemed to me that the effort to draw visible lines beyond which things get immoral leads only to confusion, and to debates as to whether, if eight inches from the floor is acceptable for a skirt length, is nine? Or questions about how loud music may be, or whether a guitar becomes irreligious if you plug it in. By resisting this kind of jugglery, I did not feel that one thereby argues for miniskirts or peek-a-boo clothes. He is merely saying that it is a mistake to try to safe-guard morals with a tape measure. Goodness and decency are dynamic things and are infinitely prior to questions about hemlines. You can dress a trull in a habit or an anchoress in a bikini, but you will not have brought about anything very significant.

I knew of institutes of advanced learning which forbade drama in the name of religion. It was all right to *read* Shakespeare and O'Neill and Beckett, but you could not act what you read. The students were allowed to produce pageants, tableaux, pres-entations, pantomimes, and programs, in which actors in costume paced about in front of sets and said lines. But you could not call it a play.

At these institutions students and faculty were not permitted to see films in commercial theaters. *Macbeth* could be shown on the campus, presuma-bly because it is Shakespeare, whose eminence places him above the strictures levelled against lesser men. One does not ask of Shakespeare's works whether there is murder and rape and adul-tery and cynicism and lies and foulness, but one does ask it of Tennessee Williams. Arthur Rank filmings of Dickens' novels were shown, but one could not go to the local cinema if it were showing the same film. It was assumed that everyone watched Garbo and Bogart and Bette Davis on television, but no one was permitted to see them or their professional descendants in the theater.

The idea here was that movies do not really contribute to a robust spiritual life. But, I thought, do doughnuts? Or roller-coaster rides? Or hootenannies? (These were not on the index.) Or, if it was objected that movies feed bad thoughts into people's minds, shall we, then, place books under the interdict?

"Oh, no—there are good books, so we can't eliminate all books."

"Are there no good films?"

"Well, yes, but if you start allowing some, you've let down the barrier, and before you know it, everybody will be in an orgy of movie going, taking in the bad with the good."

"Are they not doing that with books already?"

"Possibly. . . ."

"Well, hadn't we better interdict books, then?"

"Well, no. You see, movies represent an *industry*."

"Books don't?"

"Well, yes, but, the movie industry is a *bad* industry."

"How?"

"The actors lead such bad lives."

"Do they?"

"Yes."

"All of them?"

"Most of them."

"Do authors and publishers lead good lives?"

"I don't suppose they do."

"Well, we had better interdict books. . . ."

88

"No, you can't do that. Books are an individual matter. You can't keep people from reading Dickens just because they might then read *Fanny Hill* or *Naked Lunch*."

"But you can keep them from seeing good films lest they see bad ones?"

"Yes."

"What is your warrant for this?"

"A clear testimony against evil."

"What evil?"

"The sin of Hollywood and Broadway."

"What sin?"

"Adultery and fornication and perfidy and so on."

"This doesn't occur among authors?"

"Books are different."

"How?"

And so on. The idea was that, what with the marital intricacies of Beverly Hills and one thing and another, inasmuch as you paid $1 for a movie, you contributed $1 toward someone's Bacchanalia out there. This kind of caution did not apply, on the other hand, to other forms of entertainment. You did not ask about the extracurricular sexual irregularities of the clowns and acrobats and elephant keepers when you paid your money at the circus gate.

It was further objected that all kinds of bad things went on in films. People were forever lighting cigarettes and kissing and mixing up drinks and crawling about under the sheets. People ought not to witness these things on films. If you took exception to this method of holding the moral fort, you were understood to be suggesting that it might, after all, be a good thing for young people to start getting into bed with each other. The whole effort struck me as being a frightened and anti-rational one. It was at least anti-Christian, I knew.

The same sort of thinking occurred over the subject of alcohol. The idea was that over-drinking had brought havoc and tragedy to thousands of individuals and families and that therefore the way to register your horror at the spectacle was to abstain from drink yourself and to spread the idea about as corollary to godliness. How, it was asked, can anyone spend money on this great curse, which has ruined thousands of men and broken the hearts of their women and destroyed homes and lost fortunes? I knew people who operated rehabilitation centers for alcoholics, and their tales of human woe were ineluctable. The idea was that anything capable of working such grief in this world is in itself evil. It was shuffling to say that the evil lay in the fact that people drank *too much*. That was giving in. The strong and clear and pure thing to affirm was that alcohol was evil. We ought to hate with livid hatred anything so ruinous.

The argument was pursued on a difficult level, in that, the minute you questioned this *method* of responding to an evil, you were seen as the camel's nose in the tent. You were seen as the harbinger of all kinds of weakening and laxity and carelessness. You were understood to be suggesting that the ruin one sees on the Bowery is not, after all, so bad. You were thought to be insensitive to tragedy and horror. You were answered with earnest descriptions of human sorrow, the idea being that, given enough tragedy, you would eventually see the point. It was not at all understood that you shared fully the awareness of tragedy and that you were as distressed at the Bowery as your interlocutors. It was not understood that you deplored evil, that you deplored truckling, and that you might be as serious about goodness as your friends were. It was not understood that you, too, saw distinctions between good and evil, but that you saw them as infinitely prior to questions about *things*.

"But it's in the *things* where the evil in men's hearts has occasion to work its ruin. It's the alcohol itself that takes them to the Bowery eventually."

"The evil is in the thing, then?"

"Well, the thing is the agent of the evil."

"Could you carry this line of thinking into another realm?"

"Like what?"

"Sex."

"What?"

"Sex. It has been the cause of universal heartbreak and cynicism and murder and syphilis and suicide. All the foundlings in the world owe their misery to sex."

"Oh, but God made sex."

"But not alcohol?"

"No. That is. . . ."

"He did. Remember? And Christ made six huge pots of it at a party—*after* everyone had had quite enough. And St. Paul liked it. Had they never encountered drunkards and derelicts? Didn't that affect them? Weren't they letting down their standards by having anything to do with something that caused so much woe? And, by the same token, ought not Christ to have condemned sexual activity, since it was the occasion for half the chaos in the world?"

"Oh, but wait a minute."

"I mean, if we had been in on the Creation, and God had asked us whether or not he should make two sexes and put a great urge into both of them for each other's bodies, we would have advised him not to. We would have pointed to all the confusion and frustration and fornication and perversion and bestiality and agony that it would lead to, and we would have argued that to open up this possibility, and then safeguard the good with only some abstract strictures was foolish. Why provide the occasion in the first place? And God would have pointed out that the great mark of man was to be freedom. And so he went ahead and made things risky, and he got exactly what we told him he would get—confusion and fornication and chaos. He could have fended it off by making great barriers, but he

92

did not. For all the great and fatal risk, he insists that we be free. But his champions have always wanted to rob us of freedom and to build fences that he refuses to build."

"But if you think this way, how will you raise your children? Will you refuse to impose any strictures on them?"

"Child training is another matter. A parent is in a position to put strictures on coffee, candy, and beer, to tell the child to put on his raincoat and go to bed if it is midnight, and so on. (As a matter of fact, God used the analogy of child training in his dealings with men—but he disavowed that method as of the advent of Christ.) The problem for parents arises in the vision they give to their children as to *where* good and evil lie. And it becomes destructive when religious orthodoxy assumes the prerogative of binding its followers into perpetual childhood by preaching a morality that exists in things rather than in acts."

"So what are you suggesting?"

"That we have got to locate evil where it exists, and not elsewhere. It exists in one place only—in the heart of man. It is there and there alone that one can direct one's fervor for goodness. If you interdict films, you interdict books. If you interdict alcohol, you interdict sex. The world God made is full of risk and possibility and dynamism. It is wild and elastic and moving, and a static code of proscriptions won't do."

"Ah—I have you there. What about the Ten Commandments? *There's* your 'static code of proscriptions.' What about that?"

"Yes. What about that?"

"Well, it's positive and clear and hard. You're advocating some etiolated form of semi-morality that refuses to be bold and forbid things."

"Ask yourself just exactly *what* is interdicted in the Ten Commandments."

"Oh, there's killing, and stealing, and lying, and adultery, and swearing, and envy, and idolatry."

"Any things?"

"I just named them."

"Any *things*? Things, things, things."

"Killing and stealing and. . . ."

"Those are *actions*, man. Those are actions. *That* is where your God draws His lines. He did not tell the Israelites not to have cattle—He told them not to covet their neighbors' cattle. He did not tell them not to have sex. He told them not to commit adultery. It is that way all up and down the line. And ask yourself what is in the list of evils that Christ and St. Paul denounced? What do they see as evil?"

The whole effort looked to me like a gnostic inclination to find the dichotomy in the universe to be between matter and spirit, rather than between good and evil. This was a notion that was condemned as heresy by Christian thought, and therefore I could not see much point in urging in the name of Christian morality a scheme of things that was gnostic—that saw evil in things. One is perfectly free to do so, but one is not free to do so and remain Christian, any more than a Marxist is free to start crying up the merits of usury and laissez-faire economics and remain Marxist.

This frame of mind recalled to me the tale in the Old Testament about a well-intentioned man named Uzza who put out his hand to steady the Ark of God once when it was about to tumble off an ox cart. He did not want to see God's glory in the ditch. God killed him instantly for his pains. He struck down the only man around who cared enough to protect his glory. It seemed to me that there was a piquant curiosity here. God will not have us exceeding him in holiness. We understand him as being holy, and we want to emulate this and proclaim this, so we become solemn and scrupulous and summary and doctrinaire, and we forget that Christ came into the world and sat about with all the wrong people and made the rounds of parties and allowed himself to be accused of over-drinking, and associated with strumpets, cheaters, and fools. He did not at all fit his contemporaries' (or our) notions of goodness. We have a John the Baptist image of goodness, and the Son of Man image does not appeal to us.

Allied to this anxiety to manage morals by means of the index is the inclination of orthodoxies to appeal to certitude, and I could no longer feel that certitude was either available or desirable on the human scene. It is not a philosophical possibility.

This is not to say that passionate committal and

action are impossible. It is simply to say that one has got to recognize quite coldly that there is nothing incontrovertible about his dogma. There are a thousand vantage points from which it can be demolished. In turn, of course, one demolishes one's critics. But the business of holding a dogma is not a matter of omniscience. It is a matter of having opted for a description of things that makes overwhelming sense to you.

I felt this way about Christian dogma. I found its vision of the world and existence to be a wholly compelling one, and therefore I felt quite strenuously that alternative visions were either inadequate or nonsense. But I felt, equally strenuously, that written into human existence is something called risk, from which no human being is exempt. That is, the list of endowments granted to human existence does not include omniscience. And there is a sense in which it can be pointed out that until you know everything, you know next to nothing. The missing item might be the keystone. Christian dogma offers against this view of knowledge the notion of revelation—that God has communicated with man in terms adequate to arouse an adequate response. I did not argue with this. I shared this view. What I did not share was the notion that certitude attends the response of faith to the Word of God. It is radical risk to which faith addresses itself. Certitude assumes that risk does not exist, and this assumption struck me as whistling in the dark.

The desire for certitude is natural enough and explains the human tendency to mistake faith for certainty. This is not a specially religious mistake. We think of supernaturalism when faith is mentioned, but the naturalistic description of the world also operates on assumptions that require a faith as robust as does the most soaring mysticism. The usual efforts to skirt faith beg all the questions there are. A psychiatrist, for instance, who points out to you that you believe in God the Father because you need a father, or that you became a missionary to expiate your guilt feelings, may be quite correct, but he has not touched on the prior question as to whether there *is*, in fact, a cosmic father figure who is the archetype of all other fathers, or whether there is an evangel worth spending your life promulgating. If he does not feel that there is, then one of the items in his credo is that such information is unavailable. That it is unavailable is not demonstrable, and he must not tell you that it is. You and he give alternative readings to the phenomena of existence.

The various efforts to obviate faith by suggesting that faith addresses itself to things that are not there (corn gods, banshees, and the Man Upstairs) close down their categories at a point that precludes the possibility of any further discovery. They draw a line beyond which, they insist, there is nothing.

Religious dogma, on the other hand, periodically falls into the opposite difficulty by trying to obviate risk. It sees itself threatened by variousness and ambiguity, and hence inclines toward a posture of omniscience. It would like the faithful to feel that they have stepped beyond risk, and that things are safe and manageable now. It would like them to feel that their position has an inexpugnable validity, indeed a divine validity.

Because I subscribed to Christian dogma, I of course felt that there *was* a divine validity to it all. This was written into the case. But I could not feel that it was incontrovertible. I felt that between the serene empyrean of pure knowledge that we imagine to be the habitation of the gods and seraphim and the world we inhabit, there lies a hiatus. Certitude is one of the things, along with innocence and immortality, that has tumbled into that hiatus. So that you opt for what you believe for reasons that are far from demonstrable to human knowledge. You feel, for instance, that it is God who has brought you to faith, but then you must admit to your friends that this idea is itself an item in your prior creed. There is no escape from the roundabout in which we find ourselves. Neither the sceptic nor the priest can get outside the limits.

So that it seemed a mistake for religious orthodoxy to urge that it could lead to certitude. It affirmed faith, as all sciences and systems must, but, like all sciences and systems, it made the mistake of galvanizing that faith into omniscience. Physical science, for instance, begins by describing the world we live in, and occasionally ends up making metaphysical statements that do not at all arise from its data. The behavioral sciences begin by describing human behavior and end often by telling us about the nature of man. Religious dogma, on the other hand, claims to have a body of knowledge received from the outside and ends up by fearing and attacking half of what human knowledge uncovers.

I could not see why there should be anything so quintessentially reactionary about religious faith. But the popular religious imagination has won itself a poor reputation in human history because of this reactionism, and, where there is reactionism, it springs directly from the assumption of human omniscience.

That is, if you think you know from your sacred writings that the earth is flat (you may have read about the "four corners of the earth"), then you resist the notion that it is round and must greet the ships of Magellan with a red face when they sail into the harbor. If you know from having read about the sun and moon going round the earth that the earth is the center of things, then you must try to burn Copernicus.

It was this recalcitrance that I did not care to share. I could not see that there was any connection between religious faith and the *status quo*. My own inclination happened to be a stuffy one, and I ordinarily liked the *status quo* (or something several centuries previous to it), but I hoped that it was not for religious reasons. The minds that on the one hand resisted change and excitement and revolution for religious reasons, or that on the other saw everything new as heralding the kingdom, struck me as being naïve. I did not see that religious people were more securely placed to pronounce on revolution and new knowledge than anyone else. The hurried contemporaneity of modern churchmanship seemed as tedious as the doctrinaire obscurantism of the old.

I tended to see a threat to my gods in the arrival of the unknown. It is natural enough for us all to feel uncomfortable with the new and the strange. You cannot help but feel frightened when you think about cybernation and the population explosion and the Dow Jones average and welfarism and unidentified flying objects and life in a test tube. But your fright becomes inquisition when you feel that your god's survival depends on your success in resisting these things. It is especially odd if you say that your god happens to be the Lord of Creation.

That religious earnestness forever tends toward fright and hence toward brittleness and inquisition is clear enough in mythology and history. In the story of Job, for instance, God took the side of Job, who had complained and accused him, against Job's orthodox friends. They were correct in their propositions, but their loyalty to what they were sure was true had led them into sub-human attitudes. They had become inquisitors. Christ had a

100

similar problem with the Pharisees, and St. Paul with the leaders of early Christendom. Torquemada was a great champion of what he felt to be truth, but we do not applaud his method of guaranteeing a man's passage to heaven by cutting his skin to ribbons. But his position was logical. If you know that you know the truth and that you are in a position to decide a man's everlasting neighborhood, then to let him go on in his error is a betrayal. You must get him into heaven, whether it is with blandishments or grappling hooks.

Our own forms of inquisition are more urbane, of course. We do not dip people into pots of bubbling fat or pluck at them with glowing tweezers. We call them "bourgeois," "provincial," "obscurantist," "fundamentalist," "communist," or "unspiritual." One eager group that was active while I lived in England divided husbands from their wives and put aged aunties out into the street over points of church doctrine. Members of families ate at separate tables in the same house because they saw each other as included in St. Paul's advice to the early Church not to eat with people who taught false doctrine. A favorite practice in America was to raise a hue and cry about communism or heresy, and, in the name of the Lord, to begin all kinds of *ad hominem* assault and innuendo. I was undoubtedly too sensitive to this, in that my father, whom I had felt to be a godly and humble person, had been ignored as a fundamentalist by ecclesiastical liberals and damned as a compromiser by fundamentalists. I detested the omniscience of both sides.

The best form of inquisition, however, was the gentle one. In this situation, the inquisitor took the saintly approach. The victim was seen as having committed perfidy, either in doctrine or practice. In so doing, he had grieved the Lord and the inquisitor as well, and the latter took it upon himself to drop tears for the victim, pray for him, write him tender letters, and spread the word about that he had wandered afield. Everything possible was done to convey to the errant that he was hurting God and God's people. Any lever was felt to be legal: family ties, memories of the good old days, appeals to "the simplicity that is in Christ," and so on. It was assumed that the inquisitor's understanding of the victim's circumstances and thinking was a correct one and that he alone could point out the errors to the victim, if he would only listen.

The thing that troubled me here was that, even supposing the inquisitor to be correct, there seemed to be a violation of the *imago Dei* involved in these tactics. Suppose someone *is* going to hell. God himself refuses to violate that person's integrity in the effort to bundle him into paradise. You need not flog him in order to destroy him. You can wag your head and let it be known that he is the object of concern and prayer, until he hasn't an ounce of self-respect left. I could not see this as good. It comes to the same thing whether you are dragged nude to the pillory or prayed for publicly. You become a pariah.

The assumption of certitude did not, of course, imply that one knew all that there was to know. It involved rather a frame of mind which felt that the particular shape in which it understood its dogma was the sole correct one. This is a peculiar frame of mind in a group such as mine, which claimed to be *semper reformanda*.

The elders of all orthodoxies from the beginning of history have had to watch their sons and grandsons slide into what looked like perdition, and the tears and pleading seem to be part of the orthodox scene. Mrs. Grundy, Mao Tse-tung, Lord Salisbury and all other purists watch their allies selling themselves out to the enemy. Once, after I had been trying to explain some disturbing notion of mine to some friends, a troubled woman asked me, with fear in her voice, "What have you got—some new kind of thinking?"

I had often heard it urged that if we could just get back to the old verities and simplicities, things would come right again. It is, of course, natural to be dismayed over the way things deteriorate, and I found myself sympathetic with the defenders of any crumbling order. I was the sort of person who indulged in a great deal of nostalgia. I deplored, for instance, the disappearance of vacant lots in my home town. There had been a great corn field and a patch of woods behind our house when I was small, and it is full of tidy ranch houses and carports and playpens now. There is a bogus-colonial A & P now where some grand eighteenth-century houses used to be, and gleaming appliance shops where the old wooden bakery stood. All crossroads have given way to cloverleafs, and a great geodesic radar dome sits where a farm used to be. Everything always becomes metallic and tawdry, and the shaded streets and country roads and empty beaches of our childhood seem more and more remote, and more and more glorious.

But nothing is to be gained by nostalgia. To deplore the passing of time is to fail to come to terms with actuality, but on the other hand, to call it all "progress" is to beg the whole question as to what progress is.

The reluctance and fright that we feel about the face of the land marks our religious sensibilities too, and hence the hopeless discussions between parents and children, neither of whom can at all imagine the frame of mind from which the other is speaking. The great fear for the parents is "Where will it all lead?" and "Are there *no* absolutes any more?" and "The barriers are being broken down." It is nearly impossible for the one side to understand that change does not necessarily involve decay, and for the other to see that change is not, by definition, necessarily good.

I used to hear a man speak from time to time while I was in college, and his refrain was a winsome appeal to "the faith once for all delivered to

104

the saints." The implication was, "If we could only stick to what we have received, and keep it in the shape in which we have received it, things will be all right." Most of his hearers had lost interest in any such faith, and others were not at all convinced that the way to preserve the vibrance of dogma was to dig in. But the assumption underlying his train of thought was that the sort of religious exercise familiar to us in our sector was the grand flowering of Christian faith. If you knew God and understood his scriptures, you went about things in our way.

We had a lively awareness of the points at which all forms of Christianity other than our own failed. We were all adroit at describing how this group and that group did not quite measure up. I was once invited to describe the religious life on our campus at a regional conference of student Christian groups. I, of course, felt that the conference was a misnomer in that the other people were not Christian to begin with, since their set of priorities was not mine. In my talk I emphasized frequently what I felt to be the core of Christianity and described it as the thing that bound my group together. I do not remember what I said, but one man, in talking with me afterwards, said, concerning some point that I had made, that it did not show a great deal of self-criticism. "Not at all," I replied blithely. I thought, "Exactly. Why should we indulge in self-criticism? We have the inspired Scriptures on our side, and that's that." I felt that I had scored a point. I was congratulated by my colleagues afterwards for having given a positive word of "witness" to this misguided conference. I am happy that I do not remember the man's face now, and I hope he has forgotten both me and my remarks.

✳

In this reassessment of my religious posture I wondered in what sense it can be urged that a given segment of Christendom is exempt from the mortal threat of Ichabod. (I found this a useful term: it alluded to the Old Testament story of a woman who named her child Ichabod, because "the glory had departed" from Israel.) Biblical history was full of stories of people who were anointed ones and who finally had had "Ichabod" written over them. How did we know that the glory had not departed from us?

If this was ever suggested, we cited names from our own saints' gallery as witness to God's presence with us, and we pointed out that our people were well intentioned (they were "dear souls," "earnest Christians," and "simple folk") and we cited converts (the implication being that God was drawing the converts, and that He would not be doing this if we had not been satisfactory). We did not care to reflect that you can get converts to anything in the world or that godly forebears do not guarantee godly progeny. Nor did we stop to reflect that what is sauce for the goose is sauce for the gander, ourselves being the gander. That is, we liked the story about the people arriving at the Judgment Seat and pleading that they had done all kinds of good things in God's name only to discover that God had no idea who they were. This applied, of course, to other groups, not to us. We made a career of saying "Lord, Lord" (we are the best extempore pray-ers in the world) but never dreamed that it might be *us* to whom he would turn blankly one fine day and say, "Depart. I never knew you." We liked to tell about the parable of the branches being cut off and thrown into the fire, but we knew quite well who those branches were. We liked the story of Samson, who had been chosen by God and anointed, and who woke up one morning and tried to do great things, and "wist not that Jehovah had departed from him." We, of course, were not Samson, thank God.

We understood Scripture in a highly typological way, and were, therefore, inclined to read all stories as applicable to *somebody*. How we knew that not a word of all this was true of us, I cannot remember. It was, to our mind, not a possibility that we might be massively and tragically wrong in anything. Our patterns for devotion and worship and education and entertainment were as axiomatic as was our creed.

The unconscious assumption of certitude in dogmatic and practical matters had a curious side effect on our response to doubt. It is, of course, common, and probably fashionable, for university students to lose their religious faith. But it was not to my mind legitimate for the elders to throw out the baby (inquiry and real doubt) with the bath water (adolescent exhibitionism or dishonest doubt). At times, the official response to someone's questioning the grounds of our dogma was scandal ("This is heresy!"), or scorn ("Oh, grow up!") or grief ("You have betrayed the faith.").

But it seemed to me that the exercise of actual, as opposed to academic, inquiry, was an important and human exercise, and that the assault of doubt was inevitable upon one whose eyes are open to the ambiguities of existence. But if you attach to your loyalty to your creed the addendum that you thereby know all that is necessary to account for ambiguity and are therefore invulnerable, your faith has changed into presumption.

The tale of Job seemed to me, again, a case in point. He had a rigorous faith. It was such a great faith that God pointed him out to the devil as an example of the sort of thing he liked. But the story does not give us a very satisfactory picture of the man of faith, at least as we might like to think of him. Job despaired and complained and cursed. His experiences forced him to ask questions, not as an exercise in apologetics, but in actual and grim conflict. His orthodox friends did not in the least like this, and told him where he had gone astray. But God ended up applauding Job and not the others, even though they had been correct in what they said.

What, I wondered, was the nature of Job's experience? *God* approved of his kind of faith, but it was not a kind of faith that the orthodox mind approved of. Part of the business of being loyal to a dogma is that you manage your responses to experience so that the dogma remains intact. For instance, if you believe that the Ganges will heal you if you get into it at Benares, you don't change your belief just because it doesn't work when you try it. You say that you did not go in at the right time, or in the right spirit, or in the right position. If you find that you must go away from Lourdes or Walsingham still on your crutches, you do not rail at the Virgin: you find reasons why she did not, in this case, choose to heal you. If you believe that God protects his children, and you pray for this protection before going on a trip, and then run into an abutment and kill your family and break your back, you find ways of describing the experience so that it does not call the notion of God's protection into question. A friend of mine was killed recently in such an accident, and the publicity that went out from his home about his death described the event in terms that I should have thought applicable only to religious martyrdom. The event raised no question in anyone's mind. It would have been seen as a form of infidelity and truculence to have said, "Well, damn it all anyway." This was not how one responded to God's acts.

But it seemed to me that this was how Job responded, and he seemed to have got God's attestation. There was something sinewy about his ideas of God, whereas the ideas of his friends appeared brittle.

I thought about this friend and about another good family whom I knew who had been subjected one afternoon to murder, plunder, and rape. The response of some earnest people to all this was that we were not *allowed* the same rage, agony, and frenzy that automatically occurs to the human imagination in situations like this, because this would bespeak a faulty faith. God is good, and he had, in love, permitted it all.

I thought, right: if this sort of love is at the bottom of things, it is a strange sort of love, and no meaning that I can attach to it can make it look like what the English word love suggests. In other words, as far as our experience of life is concerned, whether things are engineered by a loving Father or by a cosmic sadist comes to the same thing. (I owed this notion to C. S. Lewis.) Clearly, Providence, in its operations toward us does not usually extend visible protection or care or amelioration or assistance—all the things we think of as being corollary to the idea of love. The Christian description of the love of God often resorts, with biblical precedent, to human analogies: filial love, fraternal love, maternal love, paternal love, erotic love. This is the imagery used to describe the motions of God towards us.

But, I thought, there is little correspondence between this idea and human experience. There are, to be sure, volumes of testimony to the joys people have known in contemplating the divine Love. St. Theresa and Pascal and Mme. Guyon and Samuel Rutherford and martyrs from all camps have exclaimed with great joy about their experience of this Love. But it is all outweighed a thousand million times by the rest of the data. There is no comparing the data quantitatively. You cannot appeal to human experience to support your notions about a loving God, for if you do, the Sadist will win every time. You will have to set the experience of a few in relatively infrequent situations against the lifelong experience of every man who has ever been born.

This emerged in my mind as the difficulty: I belonged to a tradition that affirmed the idea of Love and not havoc as lying at the bottom of things. The data of human experience lead one, however, to quite an opposite conclusion. And yet we claimed that this Love is knowable and operative—indeed, definitive—in human existence. But in our eagerness to substantiate this claim, we were forced to respond to experience with visionary imagery that often did violence to human sensibilities.

I felt that I must abandon the effort to insist on Love as the demonstrably operative energy behind human existence.

Part 3

After two years I returned to America to begin graduate study. I had been granted a teaching assistantship, not at an Eastern university, as I had hoped, but at an enormous university in the cornfields. I visited my friends in New York and Philadelphia in the interval between my arrival from Europe and my departure for the Midwest and felt I had been sentenced to exile. I walked under the trees in Rittenhouse Square and saw the dry leaves beginning to scud along underfoot and the lamplight transforming the park back into the old place where I had used to sit and where I had indulged so many unattainable and romantic fantasies, and I knew that the universities here would soon be opening, the students appearing, the bars and coffee houses filling up, and the snow falling

113

quietly past the lamps. My exile to the cornfields seemed intolerable.

I bought a sports car. It was a red classic MG with high wire wheels, a leather strap across the hood, and right-hand drive. A friend of mine who was a sociologist admired it politely, but I could see the tolerant exasperation in his eyes: "Here's Howard again. He has to have some *thing* going. If it's not a beard, it's a sports car. If it's not Europe, it's the Virgin Islands. Fur coats and astrakhan hats. Something splashy and bizarre to validate his existence."

The car turned out, I felt, like everything else in my life. Within twenty-four hours of my having bought it, it had become an incubus to me. I drove to New York, where I was to spend the night with friends and go with them the next day to their cottage on Fire Island, and on the way I discovered a bad oil leak. It was the Labor Day week end, so, while my friends went on to Fire Island, I spent a full day trying to have the leak repaired and eventually had to return to Philadelphia. So much for Fire Island.

The trouble with incidents like this was that they raised all the questions of the cosmos for me. I saw myself as fore-ordained by some malign deity to sitting out my days in garages and public health ante-rooms and cornfields, while my friends whirred by on their way to Darien, Fire Island, and Newport. I wanted to pull down the pillars of the sky one moment and to collapse whimpering the next. Why did my efforts at pleasure and bliss always miscarry? Why could I never have just one of the thousand faces that had stopped my pulse with desire and joy? Miscarriage and botch marked all my efforts. I felt truculent toward heaven.

I was not exhilarated by my trip West (I had the car repaired). As I passed the Pennsylvania Turnpike exits to Valley Forge, then Lancaster, then Altoona, I knew what other travelers had felt going east from Moscow, as they passed Omsk, Irkutsk, or Nizhni-Novgorod, en route to the salt mines.

The town that was to be my home for the next two years was a faceless one, distinguished by used-car lots, tuxedo-rental shops, and hamburger drive-ins with shuddering neon decorations. On the edge of the town lay immense shopping malls.

I moved into a modern flat with rock-hard paper-thin walls, dishwasher, air-conditioning, and aluminum window frames. It was too sterile and too far from the campus, so I moved after three days into a furnished room with a spool bed, chocolate rug, bulbous armchair, and refrigerator. I sat on the edge of my bed in the evenings and wished that the phone would ring just once.

After a month of this I found the very thing: a cellar apartment in a one-block slum near the campus. It was in a small frame house that had been carved with astonishing resource into five flats. It and the house next door were set in a tumult

115

of garbage pails, toppling sheds, mud, rubbish, and heaps of undefined compost. There was a tidy and anonymous two-story apartment building on the other side with twenty-four one-room accommodations for timid newly-weds, East Asians, and some people in psycho-linguistics.

To get down into my rooms you had to negotiate a tiny foyer with three doors: a tightly-sprung aluminum storm door, a rattling main door, and my cellar door. The difficulty of doing this with a bag of groceries was almost insuperable. The walls of the apartment were of dirty plaster trowelled over bricks in heavy relief. I painted them white to get a catacomb effect. I began to hang up travel posters and some linoleum cuts from my Norwich friend. Over the door into the living room I tacked one saying, "*Omnis spiritus laudet Dominum.*" Above my desk I put two enlargements from a photographer friend of mine (the only remotely famous person I know). Next to these I hung a tall, narrow sketch for a church window, again by my Norwich friend, showing St. Francis of Assisi bursting in ecstasy through a church roof with a hymn of praise lettered out from his head. Then an enormous brass rubbing of Sir Nicholas Dagworth (d. *circa* 1401) which I took from the floor of the parish church in Blickling, Norfolk. He loomed, black, severe, and devout, with his tilting helmet behind his head, and his dagger, broadsword, greaves, spurs, dog, and coat of arms. On another wall I hung a strange

116

semi-abstract ink drawing incorporating about a dozen church spires, Byzantine, New England, Norman, and Depression Baptist. A frantic and flamboyant interior designer friend drew it for me on an impulse one Saturday. Next to this I put a Rouault poster, and a Mondrian-like thing that a Belgian boy had given me in Brussels.

In the bookcases I juxtaposed Gabriel Marcel, *Candy*, the Monastic Diurnal, and John Updike. On top I lined up empty Riesling, Margaux, and Douro bottles, and hung some Chianti bottles from the ceiling. I bought orange and mustard burlap curtains and painted the three doors of the built-in closet indigo, turquoise, and azure, the lines between the colors *not* corresponding to the divisions between the doors. I bought a lot of arty match boxes and strewed them about, and hung up a vermilion, canary, and persimmon feather duster. I made a collage of *New Yorker* advertisements for the top of my coffee table.

The kitchen walls were a sort of flaked green chaos, and when I tried to roll white paint onto them, the plaster came off onto the roller in great dry gobs. The oven was an uncontrollable bonfire, so I had to fry or boil everything. A bullfight poster on the wall gave me the occasion to murmur my Castilian Spanish when people asked me what it said: "Platha the Toros Monumental the Mathrith." I tried to keep this part of the conversation from going further, lest they discover that that was the extent of my Spanish.

*

Life was free and kaleidoscopic and intoxicating. My circle of friends expanded geometrically, until I began leaving the phone off the hook to keep it from ringing. A strange and indefinable group of people took to gathering in my rooms on week-nights. The conversations usually lasted on into the early morning. There were a great many histrionics, as one of the pivotal figures in the group was an irrepressible mimic and clown. On week ends, I was in the habit of letting parties occur there, in that it seemed to be the largest and most accessible location for everyone. It amused me to mix the beat set with the fraternity crowd on these occasions. The rub came the next morning, when I had to shovel out the ashes and butts and collect the cans and bottles and mop up sticky pools of sloe gin from under the bed.

I discovered, without much surprise, that the governing principle behind everyone's *modus vivendi* was the hedonistic one. The university world does not differ in this respect from any other world, but there is scope in the university for a particularly dazzling form of hedonism (i.e., the sexual), in that there are, in the nature of the case, several thousand young adults living together quite free of the trammels of the parental, career, or family responsibilities that inhibit the pursuit of passion in earlier and later periods of life.

Various responses to the question of sexual hedonism became visible. It is all much less frenetic on the graduate level than on the undergraduate, in that graduates have their own apartments. There are no housemothers or monitors or roommates to outwit. There are no late minutes. People come and go entirely at their own choosing. The question becomes, then, not *whether* one goes to bed with all and sundry, but merely *with whom*. I doubt if this is an overstatement. I was at a large, isolated, ordinary university, and the week-end scene in Gomorrah could not have been more brilliant.

The most common of the responses to the question of sexual hedonism is the one that offers no argument at all. There is no defensive posture, no theory, no discussion. One goes to bed with whom one chooses simply because it is fun. Why argue? Why waste breath talking about something that is as natural and expected as eating? It is seen as a form of touching innocence even to raise the matter. I used to have morning coffee at the house of a friend, and it always interested me to see which of the three boys who lived there came down the stairs with whom. There was no more recognition of this than there was of the shoes one had on. No one asked "Who's *she*?" This would have been insufferably rural. Likewise, the principal issue at parties was the question of who would leave with whom.

Another widespread approach to hedonism was the breathless one. This line of thought, it must be said, does try to validate its activity, and it does so in the name of beauty and romance. How can anything so beautiful be wrong? These lyric idylls, the source of so much joy and fulfillment—how can anyone be so mid-Victorian as to call them ugly, or even to wonder if there is more to be said? And all the motions of life lead one eventually into bed, do they not? Especially in the spring when the ice melts, and the sap rises, the blood flows again, the sun shines on the quad, and there are ten thousand young bodies about all full of joy, *élan*, beauty, and vigor, and all bursting with desire—what do you adduce against this? To what code do you appeal for your strictures against following inclination to its end? Why not phone up some Ganymede or some Isolde and say, "Oh and it's a warm and sunlit day and I'm thinking how happy I'd be if you were here and we'd walk out together and hold hands, and sit down under some great tall tree, and your head would be on my shoulder and I'd run my fingers through your dark hair and bend and kiss you on the mouth and tell you how I loved you and my heart would be thudding with love, and instead of looking at the rest of the world with envy or disenchantment, I'd be able to look at everything with

120

joy because of my own joy. And then we could go back to my place, and. . . ." You look and see another being, luminous with all the radiance of heaven, some fair beauty, some lyric and golden form, and your heart is pierced with a searing dart and you think, "Fie on Mrs. Grundy and the bishops. Fie. Oh let's wake up and live."

A less visionary approach is the one that urges that sex is inevitable. A young man-about-Europe once said to me as he put on a scarlet-lined cloak and a mink hat and started from his London flat to find his "trick" for the night, "Oh, lots of sex. I need lots of sex." I thought, well, at least that is simple. And appealing. The idea is that, since the sexual appetite is irresistible, we may as well be realistic and face it and accept it and free ourselves from mediaeval superstitions and timidity, and accrue to ourselves as many pleasurable events as possible. It is not a frame of mind which sees itself as immoral. It simply functions without reference to what it vaguely remembers as bourgeois morality.

To established patterns of thinking this world looks like a limbo of lechery and perfidy. But make no mistake: there is a patently higher intensity of sensual delight in this milieu than obtains under more restricted conditions. It cannot be argued that the rigors imposed by accepted morality provide anything that quite equals the shifting, pulsating fascination of continual search, discovery, assignation, and gratification. In any city there are a thousand elegant people with impeccable taste in theater, wine, food, painting, and clothes, whose freedom to act according to impulse makes ordinary society look jejune. The beach-house week ends, the sandaled Saturday shopping, the Sunday brunches, the knowing glances exchanged along the appointed streets, the bars and parties and eternal newness —one wonders how the structured predictability held out by monogamous marriage wins anyone's imagination.

I used to sit in the coffee shop of the student union building at the university and watch various levels of society operating. There was the "grub contingent," who saw beards, dungarees, spinachy hair, no socks, no make-up, and non-filter cigarettes as tokens of freedom and intelligence. These people went to bed together because it was the emancipated thing to do. There were the fraternity boys, all madras and shaven and golden and lithe. They went to bed with their girls because they could not resist it. There were the open-necked, plaid-shirted farm boys who fell into bed by mistake. And there were the boys who spent hours every day up and down the hallways and stairs hunting for each other.

There is also the modern ideas approach to sexual freedom. It may be sociological: greater candor in interpersonal relationships. It may be ethical: let us abandon the tyranny and hypocrisy of traditional morality and find our true freedom in naturalness and honesty. It may be psychological: why fly from your inclinations? Why deny your own being? It may be theological: let us understand religious dicta in a new way; let us cease to pre-determine issues which are dynamic, not static. The vision of a world free from the fear and timidity and illness that accompanies established morality is an appealing one.

*

I did not get into the professional circuit in the English Department at the university. I found morning coffee in the lounge a bore, mainly because the others all knew what they were talking about and I did not. The conversations impressed me as being exercises in intellectual exhibitionism, scholarly name-dropping, and pedantic swagger. I did not have the least idea whom they were talking about when they argued about critics and editors. It had been six years since I had taken my bachelor's degree, and I had forgotten everything. I did not know about the social and professional necessities in the world of letters that make and break careers, so I never went to department cocktails.

I taught Freshman writing. When, during the preceding summer I had received information from the department about teaching, I was terrified. They seemed to assume that I knew a great deal more than I did. They asked, for instance, that we let them know ahead of time about any mimeographing that we wanted to have done. Mimeographed *what,* I wondered. I imagined my colleagues arriving on campus with great armloads of lesson plans, and I knew I would walk into my classroom with the little textbook and my class register, and nothing more. I had no idea what to expect from university freshmen. I did not know whether they would be well-read in Wittgenstein and Jaspers, or whether I would have to tell them who Dickens was.

I found that there was little to fear. The classes developed into tempestuous discussions usually, and it was amusing to field comments from jaded Chicago students on the one hand and from hopeful farm girls on the other.

One of the attendant hazards of teaching is grading essays. There were times when I despaired of knowing just what comment to make in the margin. I came across sentences like this: "This relaxing, enjoyable movie was produced with you, me, and our fellow-man in mind." Or, "How can a criminal's last words set forth a minor chaos?" Or this, about a Fellini film: "Obviously this film was designed to be viewed by a modern audience. Economic factors dictate a film is not produced for an audience of the past or one in the future. But just as obvious is the fact the whole populace will not be moved to view a film. Everyone has a point of reference in this film." I mulled over observations like this: "The sickening stupidity of war definitely holds up the greatest reflection of the nature of human sanity."

It is impossible, however, to sustain for long the notion that the pursuit of career and experience is not qualified by the conditions of existence itself. That is, you might argue that the great effort in life must be to get on with your projects and your pleasures. But there comes a point at which you begin to suspect that this assumption is assailed by actualities that destroy the possibility of any affirmation at all.

I was not suddenly disenchanted with what I was doing. My life was amusing, and my professional prospects were as good as anyone's. But you cannot reflect for long without encountering the alarming suspicion that the whole thing (existence, that is) may be intolerably absurd. For the data of existence, at least as they present themselves to our consciousness are, quite simply, paralyzing. A cold and prolonged look at it all could lead one only to terror, horror, disgust, and despair.

I wondered if this was some form of paranoia. But I did not, like the young Sartre, suppose that there were crustaceans at my heels, or that "they" were out to get me. I wondered, too, if it were merely a tedious morbidity. I thought perhaps I was being pompous and solemn. Perhaps it was infantile to come to a dead stop before questions that every man, woman, and child on earth fully aware of. But it seemed to me that even a superficial reading of existence could not possibly lead one to anything approximating optimism or affirmation.

It is possible, of course, to ignore, suppress, or fly from the data of experience. But to *reflect* on it "is to be full of sorrow and leaden-eyed despairs." Hobbes at one point suggested that life was "nasty, vile, stale, brutish, and short." Hardy thought he could detect some "ingenious machinery contrived by the gods for reducing human possibilities of amelioration to a minimum." Hopkins said what we all know, that there is no way to keep at bay "tombs and worms and tumbling to decay."

Against this awareness, the cavalier equanimity with which most of us greet existence struck me as being insupportable. A more appropriate response would be, I thought, to throw oneself from the highest tower. For the great mark of human existence seemed to me to be radical ambiguity. There was, to be sure, pleasure and hope and diversion and excitement and courage and nobility and joy on the one hand, but it was all fouled, and eventually cancelled, by blight and limitation and finitude and frustration and irrevocability and outrage and cynicism and discrepancy and grief and agony and decay and death. One may be the most blithe spirit, but one fine day one checks into the hospital never to check out again. Heroes and cads and comedians and lechers and saints and charwomen all have the lid nailed down over them in the end.

I was accustomed to hearing it said that nothing is to be gained by this line of thought. Ordinarily, of course, the source of the objection is taste or delicacy or courtesy: that is, it won't do to be forever talking of rot and Auschwitz and excrement and cancer. It is not nice. I agreed with this. Obviously the notion of delicacy is the ruling one for social intercourse, and it saves us endless embarrassment and brutality. But to carry this nice preciosity into one's vision of life did not seem at all the thing.

But I had also heard it urged in the name of religion that this line of thought would not do. "A Christian shouldn't talk like that." The idea was that, since we must argue for Joy and not Havoc as the last word, we must give the best reading possible to the phenomena of existence. Bad things must be suppressed. If you look at it all too coldly, you find things that threaten the dogma. We must at all costs insist that things are not all that bad.

There seemed to me to be an anomaly here, besides the perfectly natural confusion of delicacy with dogma. It seemed distinctly odd that a dogma which claimed to give a robust and unsentimental description of existence should feel threatened by most of the phenomena of that existence. It all looked like an effort to shore up the notion of a loving Creator by putting the best light possible on things, even if that meant stage lighting. Since it is difficult to align the notion of omnipotent Love with most of what occurs in the world, you emphasized sweetness and light as much as possible, and recoiled from the rest. For this reason you did not at all approve of stories like *A Streetcar Named Desire*, or *The Plague*, or *Another Country*, or *Rhinoceros*, or *La Nausée*. Why should we dwell on all that chaos and grief, when the Lord had made so many lovely things? Because, I felt, life is like that. Nobody ever finds the little house with the door knob made of a nut. Nobody ever gets through the tiny gate into the secret garden. Nobody ever hears the horns of elfland, or finds the faerie sea. The closest we ever get to it all is some hint or echo in a face or a painting or a concerto or a woodland glade, and then it fills us with an infinite sadness, because we know that it is lost, and that we must turn back to our traffic jams and enemas and red tape.

There was something wrong, it seemed to me, in the notion of a God whose integrity stood or fell with our ability to affirm sweetness and light. There are enclaves of joy, to be sure. But the world itself is far from being such an enclave. Human existence is marked by limitation and outrage.

This presents itself to us in a thousand forms every day. It struck me with telling force in the spectacle of the several hundred paraplegics on the university campus where I was studying. This was more than one finds at most universities, in that the campus had been equipped specially for them with ramps and elevators and buses with hydraulic

128

lifts, and they came here from all over the country. Activities had been organized for these people, and wheelchair baseball was one of the attractions. One of the teams named itself the Gimpies. I used to watch them once in a while. But I felt embarrassed and obscene standing by. There was a view possible, of course, which saw it as fun, or even funny. It was, to be sure, a heroic way to make the best of one's limitations, and a better thing than capitulation. If one is in a wheelchair, he may as well scoot around a baseball diamond as sit at home and languish. But the discrepancy between a boy's having a bronzed, sinewy, lithe body, and his having a thin, milky, feeble body seemed a hideous insult. The very possibility of fun in this situation seemed the last and insufferable irony.

I always wondered whether I was being melodramatic in my reaction to this scene, and whether the paraplegics themselves would have looked at me in pity for feeling so outraged. But it seemed to me that they had been cut off from half of what appears to make life diverting and tolerable, namely the freedom to move among one's peers, and to attract others by one's beauty or strength or talent. They may have been beautiful and strong and talented in one way or another, but they were consigned by fate to a straitly circumscribed existence that excluded enormous areas of experience. The notion of compensation struck me as being an appalling necessity.

Life seems to hold out various possibilities to us, and we are likely to imagine that in order to enjoy it to the full, we need the following things: youth, beauty, health, money, and love. Only a few have all that, so the rest of us must come to terms with existence at various removes from what appears to be the best. That is, if you are rich and healthy and beloved, but ninety years old, you know that you will be in your coffin presently. Or, if you are young and beautiful and healthy and rich, but everyone detests you, you are likely to end it all violently. If you are young and healthy and beloved and impoverished, you must settle in to the working world, and resolve your dreams of skiing in Gstaad and sailing on the Aegean and partying on the North Shore by looking at magazines and movies. If you are young and healthy and rich and ugly, whatever else you may enjoy, you must get on without the pleasure of knowing that everyone is turning to look longingly at you.

Most of us, of course, have few or none of these things, and that is why we turn to various ways of coping with the breakdown in our visions. We may build up imaginary worlds which replace the real world and in which we can feel important. We may turn to protest, and set up a demimonde of our own which does not demand what we cannot have. The Beat scene was an example of this. It held out fulfillment quite apart from the structures which established society sees as necessary to happiness, so that the penniless pariah could enjoy the same feeling of validity as does the jet-set playboy. Or we may turn to an interior world of fantasy, and talk to ourselves and to our puppy. Or we may turn to eschatological vision, seeing our own limitations as somehow leading us to paradise, while others' bliss leads them to hell.

I thought about Alexander Pope with his crazy set of stumpy little legs, and about the gnome-like Kierkegaard. I thought about Beethoven's deafness (*Beethoven's* deafness!) and wondered how he concluded that "Somewhere beyond the starry worlds, must a loving Father dwell." *Ein lieber Vater!* A cosmic djinni. I had seen a Van Gogh exhibit in the Guggenheim Museum, and looked at the scrubbed brushwork he used as he neared his dismal and demented end. I read poor mad William Cowper's "There is a fountain filled with blood, Drawn from Immanuel's veins," and thought we could all use a heaven-sent fountain of life like that. I thought about the homosexual torment of Gide and Wilde and half of the artists and musicians and poets who have ever lived. A cosmic djinni.

It seemed that one did not have to travel to Belsen to find horror. It lay on our doorsill. On Saturday mornings in New York, where I came to live after finishing my work at the university in the Great Plains, I often walk to the shops in Greenwich Village to buy cheese, bread, wine, and flowers. On the way home I pass a hospital. The thought occurs that only a thickness of brick and plaster separates the lovely tree-lined street with its Georgian houses and iron balconies from the antiseptic hush where people moan out their last hours in emaciated agony. An intruder has visited them, and they must succumb to the outrage. They have other, more important things which they ought to be doing, but someone has thrust upon them the task of dying, and they must comply. Their entire existence depended on the whim of the intruder. They have discovered the line between pleasure and doom to have been a thin one—a radically contingent one—and have found doom to be inevitable. The hilarity at a Christmas family reunion can cease instantly by a fleck of cake in a child's windpipe. Our idyllic sylvan hideaways disappear with the Caterpillar tractors and Euclid trucks of the Interstate Highway System. Our feverishly planned assignations dissolve because of late trains and traffic jams. Pleasure is at the mercy of chance. A cosmic djinni.

While I have been writing this manuscript, fifteen people have been bundled into unwelcome coffins for having been shot one morning in Texas by a boy with a brain tumor. I think they might have demurred if at breakfast they had been told they would have to lie down on the sidewalk that day because a bullet would fly into them. They might have objected that it was all too summary and unannounced. There were loose ends to be tied up and phone calls to be made and papers to be turned in and a world full of music and experience to be traveled and besides we are not in the least interested in being chosen as candidates for dissolution on this particular morning thank you very much. The long string of happenstance that led to non-being for these people made one boggle. There was no more reason for one person to be in front of such and such a shop window at such and such a moment than there was for a puff of dandelion to be sailing by. At every point in the morning he had a set of choices that might have led him differently. And at the crucial moment he might have bent to sneeze or look at a watch band. Or the assassin might have been attracted by the look of the man next to him, in which case two biographies would have been interchanged.

You cannot, of course, *remain* horrified. When we come upon suffering and blood and death it arouses horror in us, but within a few minutes of our having read about Budapest or Dienbienphu or Texas, we are back to our eggs and coffee. But we would have to admit that, according to some intolerable logic, the realistic frame of mind would be one of perpetual horror, in that there are ten thousand things occurring at any given moment that would make us shrivel. We operate, and must operate, on the assumption that if we cannot see it, it isn't happening.

✳

If limitation and outrage and chance are themselves enough to arouse horror in us, they are exacerbated by existing in a frame of radical discrepancy. That is, there is no making sense out of the wildly differing fortunes bestowed on human beings. We have a fierce and primaeval inclination toward a thing called fairness, and all the phenomena of existence do violence to this inclination.

It manifests itself early enough in our shrieking protests in the sandbox when our playmate has the shovel for longer than we do, or at the party when his piece of cake is bigger than ours. There is an energy at work in human imagination which suggests that you shall not have more than I. (It does not commonly work the other way and suggest that I shall not have more than you). But the backdrop against which all wars and negotiations, from the nursery to Geneva, from nanny to Hammarskjold, occur, is the notion of equality. It is the driving principle behind legislation and jurisprudence and collective bargaining.

But what we try to win for ourselves in human affairs by working toward fairness and equality of opportunity, and by resisting tyranny and prejudice, we do not observe in existence itself.

I live on a street, for example, that connects enormous disparities. Around the corner in one direction, Fifth Avenue leads north toward Tiffany, Bonwit, The Plaza, The St. Regis, and the best addresses in the world. In the other direction it leads immediately into Washington Square, the purlieu of students, artists, charlatans, addicts, lesbians, deviates, hipsters, and muttering old women with brown paper bags and Yorkshire terriers. Along my own block there is another world still, populated by non-English-speaking immigrants from American possessions who shop in the tinselly bargain and furniture stores that line the street.

On Saturday mornings, there is a man who comes along on a tiny platform on roller skates. He has no legs and apparently no money. He plays a miniature band: drum, cymbals, horn, and a tissue-paper kazoo that buzzes a tune when you hum into it. I often hear the march from "The Bridge on the River Kwai" coming from this ensemble.

On the other hand, a friend of mine is the chauffeur for a young French woman whose days involve alarmingly exclusive cocktail parties, gallery openings, concerts, and intimate dinners with famous people. She shuttles between New York and Paris, and her most trying moments occur, it would appear, when she must wait in the back seat of her Continental for a red light.

These are the disparities, no better and no worse than those that existed between the royal dukes and the thralls of the eleventh century. There are various ways of responding to this sort of thing. Most of us, of course, do not really mind it. We are busy getting what we can, and we cannot settle timeless social questions. Some of us positively approve of it, seeing in any change a leveling downward rather than upward. The spectacle arouses in many a furious humanitarianism, and it is this, I should think, that lies behind all efforts at amelioration through political action. Many of us can offset any serious threat to our equanimity by referring it all to an eschatological vision in which the tables are turned and all wrongs are righted.

If horror is aroused in us when we encounter what is going on everywhere all the time, terror is what we experience in the face of what is inevitable. When death is upon us, we slobber and cry out to heaven. But what is the real difference between being in a great transoceanic jet hurtling in flames toward the sea beneath, and being a few tenuous years from the same issue? In the one situation you know that you have perhaps two minutes of consciousness and identity left to you before you are blown across into nothingness. In the other you suppose, quite fondly, that you have a longer interval before the plunge. Our faculty for finding solace in this interval is a curious one. Apparently the cabins of airliners heading for the earth are scenes of wild shrieking and hysteria. What about? Death? But a minute before, as the travellers read their French phrase booklets and menus, or broke open their cardboard containers of salt, did they suppose they *weren't* going to die? What mythology enabled them to stay calm? Is there some definitive difference between death now or later?

When we hear of a woman who is finally told that she has three months to live before the cancer eats her soul out of her flesh, we are paralyzed, trying to imagine what we would do if we were she. What would breakfast look like? Would it seem worth eating? How would you see your hands, knowing that a few weeks hence a professional man would take them and cross them across your stomach to give an illusion of repose to your corpse. The choice as to where to put them would no longer be yours. How would you see your books, knowing that they would sit unperturbed on the shelves, while you thrashed out your agony on your bed, and continue to sit there after you were not? I have sometimes looked at my socks and pencils and shoelaces and it amazed me that they, worth a nickel or a dollar, would outlast me. It is an indignity.

Our situation is directly analogous to that of men in Death Row. We fill in the time somehow, but we shall not get out. The inevitable event makes the intervening activities look absurd. I have often thought that the last absurdity (whether this actually occurs or is only popular hearsay, I do not know) is the practice of allowing a man whatever he would like for dinner on his last night. What possible difference could it make whether you had had Cornish hen and Chateauneuf du Pape, gruel, or nothing? And if it did not really make any difference on that night, what about the night before that, and the night before that? You expired, that was the point, and if it was to come, then in God's name why put it off? What could possibly be the interest in passing the interval until the clock hands go round, a page is torn from the calendar, the hour arrives, and you allow the rope to be fitted around your neck? Of two corpses dangling on the ropes, what difference can it make that the one has had dinner and the other none? The interval is without significance or interest.

When I was in elementary school I used to walk home at noon, and my mother would read Dickens to me while I ate my lunch. One of the books we read was *A Tale of Two Cities*. My eyes grew round as I heard about Sidney Carton riding along in the tumbril to his death. Much later on, I wondered why one should feel especially glum on the way to the gibbet. Why is the man in the tumbril any more unhappy than the whispering bystanders? We are all in the tumbrils. We are all sitting in Death Row. One fine day the man comes, and we excuse ourselves awkwardly and disappear. How is it that our friends can go on with their checker games when they know that they are next? They are acting as though what is going to occur momentarily is entirely insignificant, yet when the man comes and calls for them, they invariably mumble, and shake, and plead. What is this? Is the summons significant, or is it not? If it is not, then why the quaking when it comes? And if it is, then whence the equanimity beforehand?

The exercises with which we surround someone's exit began to look to me like a ghastly trumpery. Who thought up the idea of tremulous electronic organ music, carpets, carnations, long cars, and slumber robes? To whom is the illusion directed? To the corpse? Do we tell ourselves that *it* enjoys the satin sheets and lead-lined copper more than a wicker basket and a trench? To us? Do *we* like the look of the pillow and the ruffled lining in the lid and the canopy over the hole at the graveyard? I knew a young mother who died hideously. After the funeral one of her children exclaimed, with an appalling effort at amelioration, "Oh, mommy's coffin had *such* a pretty satin pillow!" I thought, Sweet Jesus, no. No, no, no. Give me any day the howling wakes of Amazonia, or at least the palls, crepe, winding sheets, and knells of the seventeenth century.

If it is objected that this is morbid, and that there are other, brighter things that ought to engage our attention, then it must be pointed out that to occupy one's attention with the pretty things without reckoning coldly on doom is to be like the child clinging furiously to his pacifier while the house collapses in flames. I used to like to look at a certain periodical journal whose specialty was grainy sepia pictures of country lanes, rail fences, and corn shocks, or grandma knitting in the chimney corner while chestnuts roasted on the hearth, or Dobbin pulling a sleigh full of shouting cousins over the river and through the woods. The idea was that life was beautiful. My trouble with this was that I knew that anyone who had ever known a scene like that was by now either palsied and wrinkled or dead. You could point out idylls and pleasures until we were all black in the face, but when you had finished, I would ask that you show me one single cottage that would not crumble, one single fellowship that had not been interrupted by death, or one single face that would not crumple into lines and decay.

When I was in school and college, I was troubled by my young-looking face. I used to peer closely in the mirror to find the first softening and crinkling of the skin under my eyes. I thought that this would make me look older and suggest that I had suffered greatly (I felt that I had). My father had two deep fissures running in crescents from his nose around the corners of his mouth to his chin. I knew, since I looked exactly like him, that these would appear on my face sooner or later, and I watched for the first signs. I wanted to look slightly gaunt and world-weary.

A few years later I peered into the same mirror trying to smooth away the dark circles and creases and tissuey flesh. I watched my hairline with calipers, and tried to arrange a floppy Kennedy effect to cover my higher and higher brow. I did Royal Canadian Air Force exercises to keep from becoming pear-shaped. I eventually had to admit that a twenty-eight inch waist was irrecoverable. I watched my calves beginning to look hard and ropy. The slope down which I was clearly starting did not strike me as being in the least a delight. I failed to understand the sort of gaiety that surrounds the Senior Citizens' idea in our country. I did not mind the traditional image of age: bearded, wise, infirm, benign. I did not like the current one: shuffleboard, straw hats, Florida, fun and games, cruises to Hawaii, the hula, screams of laughter at crass high jinks, and general bonhomie. I had nothing, I suppose, against the idea of someone's playing shuffleboard when he could no longer play football. But the ethos that surrounded it all jolted me. The Senior Citizen's playgrounds looked like garish anterooms to even more garish mortuaries. I could manage the imagery of old age as a twilight; I could not accept the notion of it as a new youth, a release, or a romp.

∗

If reflecting on the limitations and disparities of existence leads us to horror, and dwelling on the inevitability of decay and dissolution leads us to terror, surely the contemplation of irrevocability can only lead us to despair.

Because our existence is subject to the tragic dimension of time, all our efforts at progress, com-

141

pensation, and amelioration become a hollow mockery. What we gain is pyrrhic, in that it is won at a cost that all but cancels the gain, and it benefits only those who come afterwards, rather than those who have struggled to win it. It is no good talking of winning wars when you have concluded them at a price that makes what you have won too valuable to touch. The Union may have been preserved in the 1860's, but hundreds of thousands of men lay rotting. The world may have been made safe for democracy by 1918, but a million men lay oblivious to what they had won, and there was no way of getting them back. The Allies may have made a heroic crawl back up the Pacific in the 1940's, but a thousand men lay in the bottom of Pearl Harbor for whom victory was a word forever without content. You can stage a Nürnberg or catch an Eichmann, but you cannot do one thing about the miles of trenches in Bavaria and Poland filled with Jewish dust. It is hard to feel any thrill about locking the barn door after every single horse has been stolen.

One summer I walked through Budapest. The broad, shaded boulevards and the bridges over the Danube and the building façades reminded me of Paris. But you could see bullet-nicks in those façades, and you knew that a thousand young students lay smothered in their graves while life in the big city went on as if no one had ever tried to break the Red rule.

In Berlin, I looked at the damp nosegays and the

142

small crosses and barbed-wire crowns of thorns and photographs marking places along the Wall. There was no discoverable reason why these people should not have made it to safety while others had, nor was there any way to help them.

And what of the irony that rewards good deeds? What of the ten thousand veterans on both sides of any war who for their pains spend the rest of their lives slippered and bath-robed up and down linoleum corridors from the solarium to the TV room? Shall we redeem their lives by sending drum majorettes and the mayor through the streets once a year? Shall we restore what the gold star mothers have lost by giving them a ride in a limousine in the same parade? Shall we remake things for the men in the cemetery by standing in silence for sixty seconds once a year? And who is sitting at expense-account lunches or in the opera box now for having saved his skin one day in the battle by cowardice, while a mate dribbles out his days in a wheelchair for his bravery?

The notion that time heals anything is a gross falsehood. Time carries us along, bringing pleasure only to annihilate it, robbing us of what we want to keep, and never returning what we would like to get back. There is no more healing for the widow than there is for the amputee. Neither husband nor limbs is ever restored. The best we can do is to capitulate and compensate, and, if possible, forget.

We call this, with heartless irony, healing. Time is the ultimately tragic dimension of existence.

＊

A reading, then, of the data offered to our sensibilities by existence, eventually arouses in us horror, terror, and despair. Horror at outrage and pain; terror over contingency and doom; and despair over futility and irrevocability. These are the conditions of our existence, and for most of them there is no escape possible under any program of human action. Social action can alleviate a few wrongs and raise economic standards, but it does not touch contingency and doom and irrevocability. Medicine can help us avoid or bear pain, but it cannot banish the possibility. Cybernetics and the behavioral sciences and linguistic analysis all examine the possibility of control over human experience, but few forms of optimism are audacious enough to envisage an escape from the conditions to which human existence is subject.

Those who do imagine such an escape become, at that point, millennial. That is, there has always existed in human imagination the vision of a realm in which the ambiguities occasioned by evil and limitation and death would not obtain. All kinds of arcadias and Elysian Fields and Valhallas and Happy Hunting Grounds and New Jerusalems are seen as the ideal against which our own existence breaks down. The vision which sees such a region is a millennial one, whether it urges apocalypse or evolution or technology as the agent. The usual thing has been, of course, to attach the millennial vision to religious dogma, and to say that God or the gods would bring it all about eventually, and that we enter that state via grace or heroism or virtue or renunciation. The vision is ordinarily one of everlasting repose, joy, freedom, and fulfillment.

This Edenic vision is not, however, one that arises except by default from the data of our experience. That is, the conditions imagined as obtaining in such an order are not conditions toward which our existence tends. They appear, on the contrary, only in unabashed contrast to what we encounter in human experience. There is nothing in our experience, for example, to suggest everlasting repose except the fact that our desires for even a limited repose here are invariably frustrated. Our nights end with the alarm clock; our week ends end with Monday morning; our holiday idylls end with the day after Labor Day. When we are given an unsolicited repose, say, by a stroke or mononucleosis or TB, our gratitude is qualified by the fact that it has been badly occasioned and will end either in death or in our having to get up again and get to work.

Nor is there anything in our experience to substantiate the notion of unsullied bliss except that such a bliss appears in contrast to our best experiences of bliss, which are brief and ordinarily chimeric. The high joy of romantic ecstasy, for example, suggests the sort of bliss which human imagination likes to think exists in Eden. But we have no experience of being either able or permitted to enjoy this level of intensity for long. Ennui or disaffection or duty or death interrupt it.

From time to time there arise, of course, efforts to see Eden as attainable within the framework of human capacities, and without reference to a context other than that which appears at our finger tips or in our microscopes. It is urged, for instance, that the religious vision of Eden is a fond one, arising from frustration and based on pathetic hopes or on a touching confidence in what does not, in fact, exist. An alternative is offered: that we construct our own Eden, using the tools at hand and refusing to cry for help to gods who exist only in our wishes. By seizing the day, by pulling together, by research, by knowledge, by effort, by charity, we can build an order that will outshine all the paradises that priests and oracles proclaim. It will be the earthly paradise, the commonwealth of love, the dictatorship of the proletariat, the great society, the technocracy, the brave new world. It will cherish no illusions about immortality. It will abolish death by affirming it. It will abolish evil by denying it. It will abolish want, discrepancy, outrage, and pain by analyzing them. This is a secularist vision.

There is, however, an alternative vision. It is the

vision of transfiguration. It does not arise from the phenomena of our existence, nor does it seek to escape them. It affirms those phenomena. It sees all of them as leading, not nowhere, but to joy.

Obviously, to suggest such a thing in the light of the discrepancies of our world, and especially in the light of the final cancellation, death, is a bold thing. Various forms of religious imagination attempt it by describing a transcendent realm of bliss and by offering methods of escape from our world into that realm. Christian vision, on the other hand, grasps the actualities of history and existence and transfigures them by seeing beyond the dark borders of finitude and discrepancy, evil and futility, doom and decay to an order that gives depth, substance, and significance to our existence.

It is a vision that affirms our world and that finds in its ambiguities not a threat, but an attestation. It seeks, not exit but redemption. It offers, not capitulation, or compensation, or negation, but redemption. And it understands this redemption to have been pivotally signaled in the Incarnation.

It is in the notion of Incarnation that what would otherwise be a brittle, fragile, and creaking structure takes on sinew and resilience and vibrance. It is at this point that Christian understanding disavows the gnostic and transcendentalist flights of religious zeal. It is here that it affirms the human condition. For it is here that the mists of Sinai, Olympus, and Asgard divide, and godhood subjects

147

itself to limitation, risk, and tragedy. And it is here that there is exhibited to the gaze of an anxious and sceptical humanity the figure of Caritas.

*

Our epoch is one that finds intense difficulty with such a vision. For most of us the difficulty arises at several points.

For one thing, the behavioral sciences have, by their analysis of human experience, brought us all to a point of self-awareness on the frontier of paralysis. Every act is explicable in terms of psychology, hence it becomes difficult to see a religious act (for example, the decision to "believe") as actually having anything to do with something external. Our awareness of our own psyche has trapped us inside it.

Further, the focus on technology in our century, and the equation of technology with progress, has led us to the belief that it *is* progress and that this forward movement extends, by a transferral of influence, from the realm of science to that of the human spirit, so that the corollary to our faith in the increase of data is a belief that we know better than our fathers did what the human condition is.

Because this idea possesses us, we are able to take a haughty view of history, seeing ourselves at the highest point in an upward slope of human development. We stand at a point beyond the hedgerows and ditches thrown across the human path for so many centuries by ignorance and credulity. Because a given era lacked a given body of information, we feel that its whole consciousness was naïve. We can, therefore, sniff at, say, twelfth-century imagery of evil along with twelfth-century notions as to the shape of the solar system. The idea is that, having come upon information that supervenes the medieval cosmology, we can thereby dismiss *all* medieval notions as merely medieval. These people had not named viruses, so they talked of vapors. They knew nothing of chromosomes, so they talked of humors. They assumed that there was more going on in the universe than human activity, so they quaintly attributed what they could not explain to ghoulies and ghosties and long-legged beasties. Their credulity left them open to the possibility of such touching vagaries as dragons, hell and virgin birth. We, of course, know better.

It is from this vantage point that we modern men can contemplate the language of religious dogma. The difficulties are at once obvious. It represents to us a set of notions that the primitive and medieval (i.e., credulous) mind found compelling, but which we no longer find to be so. We now know that nothing exists that we cannot examine through a glass or on the consulting couch.

It is because of this that we find nothing of interest in religious dogma. Its claims are 1) pre-enlightenment, 2) irrelevant, 3) dull. Against the ebullience of modern life it arrays a tedious set of propositions and strictures that are only stultifying.

We can affirm this because, in our excitement over what we are doing with our left hand, we have forgotten, for the moment, what is going on on the right.

That is, our attention is captured by the explosion of information on one hand, and it escapes our notice that the human awareness of its condition has little to do, eventually, with information. It is not our experience that information throws any finally significant light on our sense of what is at stake in existence. Einstein, Sartre, and Tillich are not more aware, for instance, of alienation and perplexity and despair than were Homer, Sophocles, and Jeremiah. Our hugely enlarged understanding of our environment and of our behaviour has not uncovered for us any *significance* in existence.

The increase in information changes, of course, our imagery for us, so that, if the Greeks could have their hero battling perplexity and threat in the form of Scylla and Charybdis, we have ours sitting in ashcans. But the increase of information does not change our sense of what is ultimately important. The human consciousness always seeks form beyond chaos. It always seeks significance beyond inanition. It always seeks redress beyond evil, and acceptance beyond guilt, and unconditioned life beyond decay. It will always understand, although perhaps at greater and greater removes, what is meant by the terms joy and freedom and splendor.

This is the stuff which is not computable. And this is what our right hand has been busy with, from the beginning of time. It has sought, with a chisel and with a pen and with a brush, to present our experience to us, and to record our timeless consciousness of form and splendor. While we have been busy with our alchemical retorts and data processing devices on the one hand, on the other we have shaped our response to existence in drama and song and drawing and dance. This is the stuff of mimetic creation.

Whatever woolly mammoths or emperors or Huns or plagues or fires were at the gates, we never ceased to subject our experience to this shaping. While our politics and industry and commerce and technology grappled with the actualities of survival and community, we always felt that what was finally significant in human life lay underneath the cluttered necessities of the conference table, the shop counter, and the drawing board. Greeks and Trojans, Tartars and Romans, Saxons and Normans, Allies and Axis all returned to their firesides and to their bards and their lovers and their wine when the armor was put off. The prime minister, the lawyer, and the longshoreman all feel that their tasks are not the last word, and that they have an identity which is prior to whatever it is they are working at.

The great irony is, of course, that what we recognize in our moments of lucidity as unimportant, eventually claims our entire attention, and we find ourselves wholly occupied with our wardrobes and cosmetics and careers and artifacts, knowing full well that these things are no more significant than our children's trinkets. But we have never been quite satisfied with this pursuit of what we knew to be ephemeral, and our dissatisfaction with this gap between appearance and actuality, or between the proximate and the ultimate, or between the futile and the significant, has expressed itself in our mimetic imagery. At Lascaux and Karnak and Halicarnassus and Angkor and Chartres and Florence and Salisbury we have figured our awe and our joy and our perplexity. Slavs and Scots and Thais and Watusi and Basques and Navajos have immortalized their passion and their ecstasy in their dances. The troubadours and jongleurs and minnesingers sang to one era, and Lotte Lehman, Elizabeth Schumann, and Tetrazzini to another. The mode changes. But the thing is the same. Joan Miró and Paul Klee do not give us the same iconography as did Rogier van der Weyden or Giotto. Marc Chagall's bucolics do not look like van Ruysdael's. The glades of Arcady and Arden are not the brothels of modern drama. King Lear does not share the vexations of Willie Loman. Beowulf and Roland are not Sweeney and Prufrock. Those old ideas of candor and valor and courtesy and romance bore us. We have our own set of images that figures for us what we feel to be notable about human existence. But the questions that lie in our imagination, and that arouse mimetic activity, remain the same, whether the imagery is ancient or modern: what shall a man do? what is the locale of evil? what is our malaise? what do we eventually want? what is significant? what is authentic? what is worthy?

The Christian vision affirms mythic and mimetic imagery. It sees here the heroic attestation by human consciousness to perfection and worth in the face of our experience of fragmentation and havoc. It sees here the human suspicion that there is an order which is unconditionally significant, and which is not necessarily or immediately apparent to technological inquiry.

But Christian vision steps beyond aesthetics when it affirms that at a point in history the mythology was actualized. Perfection and beauty became visible. Glory and truth appeared. The epiphany was, to be sure, a disappointing one. The terms were not auspicious. Nevertheless, the Christian understanding is that in the figure of Immanuel the human eye sees the final and the perfect actualization of the myth.

*

What then? Was this the announcement of pie in the sky by and by? Was it the offer of escape from the actualities of existence into a euphoric Eden where honeysuckle vines cut off the view of horror

153

and terror? Was it the invitation to join a small illuminati who would be exempted from dread and risk and anguish? Was it a guarantee of safety and warmth and certitude and predictability?

I could not think so.

But I could think that in the figure of Jesus we saw Immanuel, that is, God, that is, Love. It was a figure who, appearing so inauspiciously among us, broke up our secularist and our religious categories, and beckoned us and judged us and damned us and saved us, and exhibited to us a kind of life that participates in the indestructible. And it was a figure who announced the validity of our eternal effort to discover significance and beauty beyond inanition and horror by announcing to us the unthinkable: redemption.

It was a figure we could neither own nor manage. We claimed it as our special possession, and exacted tribute and built shrines and established forms in which to incarcerate it, only to discover that it had fled. It would not be enshrined. It was the figure of a man, and a man must live and walk with other men or die, and this man was alive. He scorned our scruple to shelter him and to prop up his doctrine. What he spoke, he spoke loudly and freely, and his words were their own defense. When we tried to help things by urging sweetness and light, or by interdicting what looked threatening, or by tithing mint, anise, and cummin, or by devising rituals and nonrituals, we found him towering above us, scorching our efforts into clinkers, and

154

recalling us to wildness and risk and humility and love. Just at the moment when we thought we had guaranteed our own standing in his good favor by organizing an airtight doctrine or a flawless liturgy or an unassailable morality, he escaped us, and returned with his hammer to demolish things. Try as we might, we could not own him. We could not protect him. We could not incarcerate him. For he always emerged as our judge, exposing our cynicism and fright by the candor and boldness of his love. He tore our secularist schemes to ribbons by announcing doom and our religious schemes to tatters by announcing love.

He appeared as a man and demonstrated a kind of life wholly foreign to all of our inclinations. For he showed us what a man's life is like when it is energized by *caritas,* and in doing this, he became our judge, because we knew too well that it is that other love, *cupiditas,* that energizes us. He told us of a city, the City of God, in which *caritas* rules. He told us that all who participate in this are citizens of that city.

We experienced this announcement as both death-dealing and life-giving. It was death-dealing because we knew our own incorrigible cupidity —the energy that makes us shriek for the shovel in the sandbox, cut into the ticket line, rush for the subway seat, display our prowess, parade our clothes, and pursue delights regardless of prior considerations.

We remembered our own torrid yearning, for instance, for other bodies, and our insistence that we must seek satisfaction at all costs because this was such an ecstatic bliss. And he said to us, yes, yes, yes, you are quite right, another body *is* the most beautiful thing in the world. This kind of congress *is* ecstatic bliss, but your unexamined pursuit of this will, irony of ironies, dehumanize you, for it is a failure to ask the questions that must be asked —questions about the *imago Dei* in you and your partner, questions about sex as a form of knowledge that requires a high warrant, questions about sex as a metaphor of realities that lie at the heart of everything, and questions about the undying notion in all of us of sex as significant and binding and most holy.

And what is true here is true in all regions of experience. Your mad pursuit is for freedom and intensity and bliss. It is natural. But, by a wry irony at work in the world, the pursuit leads you into a prison where your agony is to become more and more insistent that things shall be as you wish, and less and less able to cope with denial.

But I show you a different way. It is an alien and a frightening one. It is called Love. It asks that you forswear your busy effort to collect the bits of bliss and novelty that lie about. It asks that you disavow your attempt to enlarge your own identity by diminishing that of others. It asks that you cease your effort to safeguard your own claim to well-being by assuming the inferiority of others' claims. It asks, actually, that you die.

For, paradoxically, it offers to you your own best being beyond this apparent immolation of yourself. It says that the cupidity energizing all your efforts is the principle that governs wherever hell is found, and that the dwellers in that realm are a withered host of wraiths, doomed to an eternal hunt for solidity and fulfillment among the shards that lie underfoot. This is not your best being. You were meant to find your home in the City of God, which is among you. Here duty is ecstasy. For that is what is meant by *caritas:* it is the freedom which follows upon the capacity to experience as joy what you are given to do.

But the City is not reached in a moment. It is as remote as the Towers of Trebizond, and as near as your neighbor.

And we experienced his announcement as death dealing again, because it knocked over all the little pickets and wickets that we had tapped carefully into place to guarantee the safety of our religion. He saw our masses and rosaries and prayer meetings and study groups and devotions, and he said yes, yes, yes, you are quite right to think that goodness demands rigor and vigilance and observance, but your new moons and sabbaths and bullocks and altars and vestments and Gospel teams and taboos and Bible studies are trumpery, and they nauseate me because you have elevated *them,* and I alone am the Host. Your incense is foetid, and your annotated Bibles are rubbish paper. Your meetings are a bore and your myopic exegesis is suffocating.

Return, return, and think again what I have asked of you: to follow justice, and love mercy, and do your job of work, and love one another, and give me the worship of your heart—your *heart*—and be merry and thankful and lowly and not pompous and gaunt and sere.

But we experienced the announcement as life-giving because it was an announcement, appearing in a dirty barn, and heard among the dry provincial hills and then in the forum of Rome and in the halls of royal princes and in the kitchens and streets of Paris and Calcutta and Harlem and Darien, that Joy and not Havoc is the last word. It announced to us what we could not hope. It saw limitation and contingency and disparity and irrevocability and mutability and decay and death, and it said yes, yes, yes, you are quite right: terror and horror and despair are the only eventually realistic responses . . . *if* this is all there is to it. But it is not.

You have thought of a world free from such conditions. In all your imaginings, and in your myths and your mime and your songs and dances and epics—in your quest for form and significance and beauty beyond fragmentation and inanition and chaos—you have bespoken such a vision. I announce it to you. Here, from this stable, here, from this Nazareth, this stony beach, this Jerusalem, this market place, this garden, this praetorium, this Cross, this mountain, I announce it to you.

I announce to you what is guessed at in all the phenomena of your world. You see the corn of

158

wheat shrivel and break open and die, but you expect a crop. I tell you of the Springtime of which all springtimes speak. I tell you of the world for which this world groans and toward which it strains. I tell you that beyond the awful borders imposed by time and space and contingency, there lies what you seek. I announce to you life instead of mere existence, freedom instead of frustration, justice instead of compensation. For I announce to you redemption. Behold I make all things new. Behold I do what cannot be done. I restore the years that the locusts and worms have eaten. I restore the years which you have drooped away upon your crutches and in your wheel-chair. I restore the symphonies and operas which your deaf ears have never heard, and the snowy massif your blind eyes have never seen, and the freedom lost to you through plunder, and the identity lost to you because of calumny and the failure of justice; and I restore the good which your own foolish mistakes have cheated you of. And I bring you to the Love of which all other loves speak, the Love which is joy and beauty, and which you have sought in a thousand streets and for which you have wept and clawed your pillow.

*

So there is this, I thought, as an alternative to despair. At least it is not meliorism or optimism. But

159

the *peril* of staking everything on this kind of vision . . . Incarnation. Redemption. These are far from verifiable, and this is ridiculous in an age that insists on verification.

And *caritas*. This is impossible. How is a man to opt for a kind of life in which he stands to lose everything? I mean, if you want to get a seat on the subway you have to push for it. *Tant pis* for the one who has to stand. And if you want the ecstasies, you have to go flat out to accumulate them. How can a man be expected to opt out of everything that looks important on the chance that there is more to it all than meets the eye? It is too great a risk.

Perhaps that is what is asked, I thought. Perhaps there is no escape from risk. Perhaps there is no explanation offered for the staggering ambiguities, nor any answer given to the agonizing questions. Perhaps a man is asked to opt with all his might for authenticity. Perhaps the great thing is to respond, with as much integrity as he can summon, to the cues. There *are* some—in his own consciousness, in his art, in his world. And there is this great light that has appeared in the murk, like a morning star. It is there, silent and glorious. An odd road marker. But perhaps a man is asked to go that way on the supposition that it is not all a ghastly cheat.

Yes. Perhaps that is what is asked.

DATE DUE

JUL 21 1969			
AUG 12 1969			
SEP 22 1971			
GAYLORD			PRINTED IN U.S.A.